W9-BCR-633

Hoover Institution Publications

THE BRIDGE AND THE ABYSS

The Troubled Friendship of
Maxim Gorky and V. I. Lenin

Published for
THE HOOVER INSTITUTION
on War, Revolution and Peace
Stanford University · Stanford, California

THE BRIDGE
AND THE ABYSS

The Troubled Friendship of
Maxim Gorky and V. I. Lenin

by BERTRAM D. WOLFE

FREDERICK A. PRAEGER, *Publishers*
New York · Washington · London

The Hoover Institution on War, Revolution and Peace, founded at Stanford University in 1919 by the late President Herbert Hoover, is a center for advanced study and research on public and international affairs in the twentieth century. The views expressed in its publications are entirely those of the authors and do not necessarily reflect the views of the Hoover Institution.

891.78
W855

FREDERICK A. PRAEGER, PUBLISHERS
111 Fourth Avenue, New York, New York 10003, U. S. A.
77–79 Charlotte Street, London, W.1, England

Published in the United States of America in 1967 by Frederick A. Praeger, Inc., Publishers

© 1967 by Bertram D. Wolfe

All rights reserved

Library of Congress Catalog Card Number: 67–27953

Printed in the United States of America

Oh martyrs of Russian literature! As before it is given to gendarmes and policemen to be the first critics of a writer's work.—SVETLANA ALLILUYEVA

To all those who, knowing this, have continued to write, this book is dedicated.

64863

Foreword

For reasons having nothing to do with literature, in the years of his decline Maxim Gorky was overpraised, his spirit misrepresented, and the worst of his works exalted as models for other writers and literary masterpieces. By way of reaction to this false exaltation of his declining years spent under Stalin's harsh rule, many who loved Russia and suffered life-long exile for her sake have tended to misprise him. As a writer he was neither the "genius of proletarian literature" that Stalin's powerful propaganda apparatus acclaimed him to be nor the fabricator of the straitjacket called "socialist realism," nor the mere minstrel of the forced labor construction camps of Belomor that some critics in exile have tended to reduce him to.

His complexity sprang from an ambivalence of spirit which caused him to oscillate all his life between the quest for truth and justice and the longing to believe in the salutary lie and its supposed power to make men better by mere insistent repetition.

Even under Stalin, who lured him back by the promise that he might leave again for Italy whenever his ailing lungs required it, this ambivalence continued. As the world well knows, Maxim Gorky died two deaths: the first on June 18, 1936, with elaborate medical accounts of its causes in the press, and with all the pomp and circumstance of a state funeral as the greatest genius of proletarian letters. The second death was reported in March 1938, eighteen months after the first, when the former Secret Police Chief, Yagoda, and Gorky's doctors, Levin and Pletner, were compelled to confess at a show trial that they had caused his demise by prescribing false medical treatment. Actually this weird charge had some substance, for Stalin himself had ordered Yagoda to have his doctors tell Gorky that not Italy but the Crimea was what he needed for his tubercular lungs.

The suspicious Stalin had learned by 1934 to distrust Gorky, for the all-powerful dictator failed repeatedly to extract from the stubborn and morose Gorky a eulogy similar to the *Memories of Lenin,* written upon Lenin's death. That Stalin's suspicion was justified became clear when the dead writer's home was searched after his funeral and hidden notes were turned up which caused the then Secret Police head, Yagoda, to say: "No matter how well you feed the wolf, he still dreams of the woods."

This pathetic story of the years of Gorky's decline and his attempt to adapt himself to and secretly to moderate Stalin's brutal rule shall be reserved for telling on another occasion. In this study I wish to limit myself to the years of Gorky's most creative period, to appraise his stature as a writer by selecting that part of his work which stands up as literature, and to throw some fresh light on his character in the years of his freedom by examining the peculiar ambivalence of his troubled and frequently stormy friendship with Lenin. What emerges, I hope, will be a better understanding of the true character of Maxim Gorky as man and artist than hagiographers or denigrators have given us, and, since this is the only artist and non-politician with whom Lenin preserved a life-long friendship, fresh light on Lenin as well.

Acknowledgments

I am indebted to the Hoover Institution on War, Revolution and Peace for the research fellowship which made the writing of this book possible. In addition, the Hoover Institution made accessible its own excellent library, the library of Stanford University, the generous help of their respective librarians, and valuable special collections and archives, including hitherto unpublished letters in Gorky's own hand. I owe to Anna M. Bourguina, Curator of the Boris I. Nicolaevsky Collection, the holograph of Maxim Gorky's letter to Anatole France, and to Rita Campbell, Curator of the Hoover Archives, the original letters of Gorky to Herbert Hoover and the American Relief Administration and the cable of Hoover to Gorky, used in the present volume. Among the librarians who gave unstintingly of their help, special acknowledgment is due to Marina Tinkoff, who read this work in manuscript and whose knowledge and love of Russian literature and enthusiasm for Maxim Gorky were a source of continuous suggestions and stimulation.

In the Hoover Tower, too, I found scholars with kindred interests with whom I might talk out problems as they arose. Among these I owe an especially great debt to Richard Wraga, who read the manuscript, advised me on the bibliography, and, with his profound knowledge of Russian literature, Russian intellectual history and Gorkyana, helped at many junctures in my work.

Others who helped when called upon were Mrs. Xenia Eudin, Gleb Struve, and on the poet Gumilev and the so-called Tagantsev Conspiracy, Boris A. Fillipov and the poet and friend of Gumilev, Irina Odoevtseva.

In thanking them for their help I do not wish to imply any responsibility on their part for my final judgment or for any defects that may appear in this book. Finally I wish to thank Olga Bellermann, Heide Meckel and Ann Rae Richard for their patient typing and retyping of the manuscript and their help in preparing the bibliography, and Carole Norton for her thoughtful editing.

BERTRAM D. WOLFE
The Hoover Institution
Stanford University

Table of Contents

List of Illustrations

THE BRIDGE AND THE ABYSS

The Troubled Friendship of
Maxim Gorky and V. I. Lenin

CHAPTER I

The Poet and the Politician

Between Lenin and Gorky yawned an abyss. Over it was thrown a bridge of friendship and admiration—genuine friendship I think on both sides, and genuine admiration. But the bridge was as insecure as a rope bridge over a rain-forest canyon. Since in Lenin's words, "friendship is friendship and duty duty,"[1] and since indeed each held duty higher than friendship, the fragile bridge was constantly breaking and falling into the abyss.

Like the friendship and the admiration, the abyss was genuine too, and so deep that it is hard to exaggerate the difference between these two men: in temperament, in outlook, in conception of man and his fate; in feelings about politics and organization; in attitude toward the autonomy of the artist in relation to classes, parties, and organs of censorship and control; in their views of the role literature and art should play in the informing and shaping of life; in what, for want of a better term, we may call the religious faiths of the two men.

Gorky had a downright distaste for politics; Lenin was infatuated with it. Despite a weakness for didactic interpolation into his tales and plays and for garrulous sermonizing in his old age, Gorky was all artist. Despite an affectionate memory of the literary classics he had read in his youth, Lenin was all politician. Lenin believed in classes, class struggle,

[1] Letter of Lenin to Gorky, January 1913. Lenin, *Sochineniya*, 4th Russian edition, Vol. XXXV, p. 44. Unless otherwise noted all quotations from Lenin are taken from this edition, which will hereafter be referred to as *Lenin*. With these words Lenin was giving fresh currency and meaning to an old Russian proverb.

3

dictatorship, the Party, and himself as the maker and mover of history. Gorky believed in Man, in freedom, in the redeeming power of art and science, in the sacredness of the individual person. When Gorky let his didactic propensities run away with him, Lenin was furious, not because the moral marred the fable, but because it was usually from Lenin's point of view the wrong moral. The ideas at the core of Gorky's thought and creation were to Lenin an abomination, and he told the author so in many an explosive letter and disapproving conversation. But as a rule he was careful not to attack Gorky in public. To Inessa Armand he could speak of the writer scornfully as "the little calf." To Shlyapnikov he wrote, "What a pity that Gorky dishonors himself by signing the filthy scrap of paper of those miserable Russian liberals" (referring to an open letter of artists, writers and actors against German wartime atrocities) ; and again, "Gorky is always quite characterless in politics and surrenders himself to feelings and moods." But when on one rare occasion he did reprove Gorky publicly because the latter had written an open letter to the Provisional Government calling upon it to strive for an early and honorable peace, he was careful to preface his strictures with a tribute: "There is no doubt that Gorky is a gigantic artistic talent who has been of great use and will be of great use to the world proletarian movement. But why does Gorky mix in politics?"

Gorky, for his part, was gentler with Lenin when he reproved him in private correspondence, yet no one criticized Lenin more sharply in the press for overt acts which the artist considered harmful or inhuman. In the most crucial years 1917 and 1918, when Lenin was seizing power and exercising it according to his fanatical dogmas, Maxim Gorky criticized the Bolshevik leader scathingly day after day in the most popular paper in Russia, *Novaya Zhizn,* whose publisher and editor-in-chief was none other than

Gorky himself. All the second half of 1917 and the first half of 1918, this drumfire of criticism continued to be so sharp, direct, accurate, and stirring that Lenin finally closed down the paper by force, after various devices of covert harrassment had failed.

The huge propaganda apparatus of the world's most powerful state has so overlaid the true picture with legend that the average educated man, not only in the Soviet Union but in other lands as well, does not know of the existence of these differences. It is the purpose of the present study to scrape off the various layers of over-painting in order to restore something of the true image of Maxim Gorky as artist and passionate thinker, and to make clear the complex, uneasy nature of the friendship of Gorky and Lenin.

Soviet scholars, on order, have suppressed some of the most important and characteristic parts of Gorky's life and work. From 1949 to 1955 they published what purported to be the complete works of Maxim Gorky in thirty volumes, sponsored and edited by the Gorky Institute of World Literature. But one looks in vain in these thirty volumes for the striking little book of articles first written against Lenin in 1917, then collected from Gorky's signed columns in *Novaya Zhizn* and republished as a pamphlet in 1920 under the title *Revoliutsiia i Kultura (Revolution and Culture)*. Omitted too is the no less striking and characteristic *O Russkom Krestyanstve (On the Russian Peasantry)*, published by Gorky in Russian in Berlin in 1922. Like Zamyatin with his *We* and Pasternak with his *Doctor Zhivago*, like Sinyavsky and Daniel and Yesenin-Volpin, Gorky had to publish these works abroad. His publisher was the Russian socialist publishing house in Berlin of I. P. Ladyshnikov, which had published many of Gorky's works in Russian in Berlin because they could not be published in his own land under Nicholas II, and which now was called upon by Gorky to do the same thing for works he could not publish in the new Russia ruled by his friend Lenin.[2]

Between 1958 and 1960, the Soviet Academy of Sciences and the Gorky Institute of World Literature jointly published in four solid volumes a "scientific," i.e. scholarly, *Letopis Zhizni i Tvorchestva A. M. Gorkogo* (*Chronicle of the Life and Creative Work of A. M. Gorky*—hereafter referred to as the *Chronicle*), purporting to set down and briefly characterize day by day every event in Gorky's life from birth to death, every letter sent or received, and every scrap of writing from his pen. Here the articles Gorky wrote against Lenin in 1917 and 1918 and collected in 1920 for the little book against the Bolshevik seizure of power, are recorded individually by title and date of first newspaper publication—but with no summary or excerpt, nor any hint that they were directed against Lenin, or that Gorky still felt strongly enough about them to make a book out of them in 1920. The book itself is omitted from the *Chronicle,* as it was from the *Collected Works.* Whereas other titles get a line or two of explanation, quotation or comment, for these articles only meaningless dry bones of titles are given.

How can one know from the entry for January 9, 1918, which reads " '9 January–5 January,' *Novaya Zhizn,* No. 6," that this is a devastating comparison of the firing of the Tsar's troops on unarmed workingmen on January 9, 1905 ("Bloody Sunday") with the firing by Lenin's Red Guard upon unarmed workingmen on January 5, 1918, as they

---

[2] Gorky's collected works bear the title *Sobraine Sochinenie v 30 Tomakh* (Moscow: Institut Mirovoi Literatury im. Gorkogo, 1949–1955). The reader is given to understand that with Vol. XXX, *Pisma, Telegramy, Nadpisi (Letters, Telegrams, Inscriptions)*, published in 1955, all the last odds and ends are included. There have since been a number of additional letters and archives published, but neither *Revolution and Culture* nor *On the Russian Peasantry* has been "rehabilitated."

marched under red banners to greet their elected representatives and honor the Constituent Assembly?

Or how can one tell from the colorless entry of July 16,
1918, "Closing of the Journal, *Novaya Zhizn*" (an entry
documented in pseudo-scholarly fashion by citing another
journal which reported the shutdown the following day),
how can one guess that it was not Gorky who closed his
journal, perhaps for lack of funds or loss of interest, but that
the shutdown was ordered by Lenin and enforced by his
police? The more one examines the flood of Gorkyana—
Collected Works in various editions; volumes of *Gorky
Archives; Selected Works* and individual works; *Correspondence* and *Literaturnoe Nasledstvo*—the more such gaps appear.

To take only one example, there is the sensitive matter of
Gorky's attitude toward the United States. When he visited
New York in 1906 to raise money for revolutionaries, his
mission was frustrated and his life made bitter by the Tsar's
ambassador, who let reporters know that the actress who
accompanied him, Maria Fedorovna Andreeva, was not married to him, and that he had a legal spouse, Ekaterina
Pavlovna Peshkova, in Russia (the couple had amicably
separated but never been legally divorced). Since Gorky
wrote with his heart rather than his head, in his anger he
published a series of bitter attacks upon the United States,
with the striking conclusion, "I could write a million words
about America and not one good one among them." But
when America aided Russia's starving millions unstintingly
during the great famine of the early 1920s, Gorky wrote,
again as his heart bade him, moving words of praise and
gratitude to Herbert Hoover and the American Relief Administration of which Hoover was chairman. On July 30,
1922, for example, he wrote Hoover a letter telling him how

many millions of children's lives he had saved, how many thousands of students, how many hundreds of intellectuals.

> In all the history of human suffering [he concluded] I know of no accomplishment which can be compared in magnitude and generosity with the relief that you have accomplished. . . . The generosity of the American people resuscitates the dream of fraternity . . . at a time when mankind greatly needs charity and compassion. It will be inscribed in the pages of history as unique, gigantic, and glorious . . . and will long remain in the memory of millions . . . whom you have saved from death. . . . The recollection of American self-sacrifice will make these same children better, more generous men and women. . . .

This is not only good Gorky prose; its publication alongside the *City of the Yellow Devil,* republished by the Russian Government so many times in so many languages, is an elementary necessity for a complete picture of Gorky's mind and heart as well as of his view of America. Yet this, and a companion letter calling the field workers of the A.R.A. "heroes who so splendidly do their work on the vast fields of death, amidst epidemics, savagery, and cannibalism," have never been published in Russia.[3]

Such is the editing in Russia for scholars and by scholars of Gorky's life and work. Nor are the scholars to blame, many of whom are devoted men dedicated to literature and schol-

---

[3] The first of these letters is in the possession of the Hoover Institution, Stanford University, and the second was published for the first time in *Novyi Zhurnal* (New York), Vol. LXXXII, 1966, 285–87. The only reference to the Hoover Commission in the four-volume Gorky *Chronicle* is an entry under date of July 25, 1921, saying that Hoover telegraphed offering aid and "putting political conditions." It does not suggest that aid was given or accepted, or that Gorky expressed gratitude or wrote these letters, but merely adds ironically that part of Hoover's telegram was used in an article in *Krasnaya Gazeta* on August 11 under the heading "The Greek Hoover and His Gifts" ("Danaets Guver i ego dary"—the epithet *Danaets* being derived from Laocoon's warning concerning the Trojan horse, *Timeo Danaos et dona ferentes.)*

arly truth. But on every literary collegium there is a representative of the Party and the police. On doubtful matters the rule is "one man, one vote," and the one man that has that vote is the representative of the party and police.

For the general reader, matters are made even simpler. Thus, on the ninetieth anniversary of Gorky's birth, *Literaturnaya Gazeta* told us:

Gorky unremittingly upheld the principle of combative, highly ideological (*vysoko-ideinii*), party-spirited (*partiinyi*) literature with all the passion and conviction of an artist who had linked his fate with the Communist Party and put his mighty talent at the service of the Soviet people, the Soviet State.

Still more popular accounts assert that Gorky was "formed as a writer by the revolutionary movement organized by Lenin and Stalin" and was a "lifelong friend and comrade-in-arms" of each of these two leaders in turn.[4]

This is the official legend which, by dint of the volume, noise, and persistent power behind it, has prevailed not only in Russia but also abroad,[5] over the more human and complex truth.

[4] See the article on Gorky in the *Bolshaya Sovetskaya Entsiklopediia,* 2d edition, Vol. XII, sent to press May 28, 1952, pp. 245, 255.

[5] The *Encyclopedia Britannica* in its article on Maxim Gorky (Vol. X, 1956, p. 532) says: "In 1917, he gave his support to the Bolsheviks," though 1917 and 1918 were the years of his bitterest opposition to Bolshevism. The article was written in America by Prince Dimitri Sviatopolk Mirsky, an honest writer on literary matters who was obviously taken in by the general hullabaloo coming at that moment from Russia under the rubric "Gorky is with us."

CHAPTER II

Out of the Depths

In the middle 'nineties of the last century Maxim Gorky shot up on the horizon like a rocket from a submarine. Suddenly, from the lower depths, or as one critic put it from "the dregs of society," came a man who had lived as a part of the underworld and could write about it. Dressed like an Old-Believer merchant from Central Russia; with walrus mustache and strongly chiseled face; his spirit passionate; a romantic, sentimental, sensitive man, swift to tears, modest and shy in the presence of men of letters; noisily assertive, even rude when faced by a throng of admirers—here was a being who had lived in the world of vagabonds, tramps, broken-down pilgrims, bums, prostitutes, part-time thieves, beggars, migratory workers, and assorted poor of the slums and riverport jungles of the mighty River Volga. Now, with two or three remarkable short stories and the advice and encouragement of a couple of men of letters, he suddenly broke through from the underworld and migratory life in which he had lived for the preceding five years into the world of books and culture of which he had never ceased to dream. Other writers before him had written of this nether world, but none had seen it from within, nor regarded it with his unflinching curiosity. To the educated Russian, this tramp suddenly become a man of letters was truly a sensation.

Russian society was in a mood to make a cult of the vagabond writer from the lower depths. The educated world was uneasy about its material well-being and lack of moral passion. The cult of the peasant having petered out, a new object of sympathy was being sought, a new class crying aloud for redemption and possessing the power to redeem. It was not unnatural that men should mistake this artist from the world of tramps and outcasts for a "proletarian writer," and his personages for "proletarians."[1] Lenin was not alone in making this mistake.

But if Lenin was not alone, it was he who canonized Gorky as the "greatest proletarian writer" in a polemical article written in 1910, and published at a moment when Gorky had lined up with the dissident Bolsheviks, Bogdanov, Lunacharsky, "and Company," whom Lenin had just read out of his organization. These words became a sacred text on which all Soviet criticism of Gorky was to be based, although Lenin had written them not for the purpose of exalting Gorky but to denigrate his associates. When Gorky broke with Lenin, "the bourgeois press" (such Socialist dailies as *Vorwärts*) wrote that Lenin had "expelled Maxim Gorky." In his own journal Lenin said in reply:

Indeed, there is no point in concealing the fact . . . that M. Gorky belongs to the supporters of the new group. Gorky undoubtedly is the greatest representative of *proletarian* art, one who has done much for it and may yet do more. Any faction of the Social Democratic Party may justly be proud of his belonging to it. But on that basis to put into its *platform* "proletarian art"

---

[1] Of course, not all Russian intellectuals thought of literature in the clichés of class and social content. Thus Angel I. Bogdanovich, the Editor of *Mir Bozhy (God's World)* wrote in a review of Gorky's first two volumes of *Sketches and Tales:*

Most of Gorky's stories breathe the freedom of the steppe and the sea. One feels in them a buoyant mood that distinguishes them sharply from the stories of other authors who have been touched by the same world of beggars and outcasts. This mood is transmitted to the reader and lends the stories the charms of freshness, novelty and vital truth. (*Mir Bozhi* No. 7, July 1898.)

means to give that platform a certificate of poverty, means to reduce its group to a literary circle. . . .[2]

But whatever Gorky may have felt moved or compelled to say twenty years later in Stalin's Russia, during his entire creative period he thought of art as human and classless. Moreover, the men and women of whom he wrote were not industrial proletarians at all. Nor did they fit into any of the legally or socially defined estates of traditional Russian society. They were outsiders, existing below the world of the official estates, some of them thrust into the lower depths because they had been cast out by society in rapid transition from cottage handicraft to factory industry, but the majority there of their own free will because they were men and women who could not or would not fit into the humdrum workaday world. The characters whom Gorky watched and listened to so intently and whose life he had been sharing included gypsies; gamblers; petty swindlers; beggars; degenerate versions of the *strannik,* the holy wanderer or fool of God; ruined gentry; ex-peasants and bankrupt artisans; self-deceiving dreamers expecting any day to escape from the depths into which they had sunk; fugitives from justice driven into outlawry perhaps by a single, even a justifiable crime; feckless vagrants who preferred to work briefly only when hunger or thirst for vodka forced them to; thieves—professional thieves as well as thieves-of-occasion, who stole from each other or, while working on some odd job, carried off with them everything not locked up or nailed down and

[2] This was published in Lenin's journal *Proletarii* on March 6, 1910, and in *Lenin,* Vol. XVI, pp. 183–87. Lenin was engaging in a debater's trick, for it was Bogdanov, not Gorky, who had elaborated as one of his own pet doctrines the theory of a purely class "proletarian art." Long after this particular squabble was forgotten, as so often happens in Lenin's continuously polemical writings, the pronouncement remained, to become a critical axiom of Soviet thought and to be developed by exegesis into a whole body of doctrine on the possibility, the content, and the prescribed style of "proletarian class art."

traded it for a single vodka binge; wandering ex-students and ex-soldiers who had come down in the world; all the misfits and rebels against tradition—in sum, all the flotsam and jetsam of a society which had no use for them and for which they had no use.

Gorky looked on the companions of his wanderings with sympathy, understanding, and admiration. He romanticized their impulsive deeds. He thought much more highly of them than of the artisans and peasants he had known. As long as they were young and strong and fearless, they were heroes for his tales, embodiments of his cult of the strong-willed, the courageous and the free. "I liked their anger at life," he wrote, "their mocking hostility toward everything and everybody, and their carefree attitude toward themselves."

They were men and women who so loved their freedom from the restraints and injustices of the conventional world that they were ready to plunge into the lower depths of life in order to attain its precarious freedoms. They bore bravely or indifferently its negative aspects—uncertainty, privation, solitude—triumphing over them and retaining in greater measure than the men of settled life he had known, the ability to jest, sing, philosophize, discuss the existence of God and the meaning or meaninglessness of life, to dream of better things or of attaining the unattainable. Though they existed as naked, homeless, hungry and thirsty animals, they yet remained *Men*—a word which Gorky always wrote with a special reverence and was prone to spell with a capital M.

He was sure these things were so, for he had lived among them and with them; shared their hazards; listened to their sober and drunken talk; heard from each his life story and how he came to the lower depths; witnessed as an aloof but fascinated observer their thievery and debauchery; marked their quips, jests, obscenities, blasphemies, pieties, illusions,

dreams; watched them with an admiring and insatiable curiosity, noting everything down indelibly on the tablets of his
memory.

All his best stories, and his one good play, appropriately
entitled *Na Dne* (*At the Bottom*), have as protagonists the
actual men and women he had known in this world, their
lives as they had told them to him, their views, conversations,
feelings—transposed only by being filtered through his
poetic, romantic and sentimental imagination, and subjected
to the selection and unification which make raw experience
into a work of art.

His tragic figures were from the same company as his
heroes: the strong men of yesterday seen in premature old
age, sick, apathetic, will-less, defeated by life, bereft of illusion, disintegrating amid the bare and dismal surroundings
over which yesterday they had triumphed. How swiftly decay
came in this hard world!

It did not occur to Gorky to hold "society" responsible for
the vagabonds he had met and put into his stories. Later,
when literary-political mentors tried to get him to do so, he
did it lifelessly, producing cold, mechanical stories, over-
loaded with pompous, didactic excursions that followed from
neither character nor plot.

But the last words of an Orlov, who rises from the airless
filth of a cobbler's cellar-hole to the exalted post of sanitary
worker in a hospital and then throws it all up for the meaningless, boundless freedom of the tramp, are much closer to
Gorky's vision of the vagrants he knew:

So after all [says Orlov] I never accomplished any heroic deeds.
Yet I still long to distinguish myself—to reduce the whole world
to dust . . . to beat up all the Jews—it's all the same to me! . . . I
was born with unrest in my soul, and my fate is to be a tramp. I
have wandered everywhere but find no comfort. . . . Vodka

quenches the heart. As for towns, villages, people of different
sorts, I find them all revolting.[3]

In short, Gorky's protagonists were anything and everything except an organized class or a part of organized society.
Far from being that "industrial proletariat" on which Social
Democracy based its vision of the future and in which Lenin
saw the compact, organized force to help him batter his way
into power, rather were they part of what Marx had scornfully called the *Lumpenproletariat*.

In 1905, such types were actually recruited by the police to
form the drunken hooligan mobs that beat up "Jews and
students." If in 1917 and 1918 Lenin was able to use them for
his purposes, it was because many of his inflammatory slo-
gans, such as *Grab Nagrablennoe!* (Rob what has been
robbed!) or his calls for "street justice," were pitched close to
the level of hooliganism. But in 1903, when Gorky protested
the Kishenev pogroms and raised an accusing voice against
police and government, the conservative Burenin wrote in
Novoe Vremya that Gorky could not escape his own share of
the blame, since those who carried out the pogroms were
Gorky's own favorite heroes, the Chelkashes, Konovalovs,
and Orlovs of his stories. Gorky withdrew the phrase about
"beating all the Jews" from subsequent editions of *The
Orlov Couple,* but the closing speech of Grigory Orlov as
originally given shows how vivid and true was Gorky's vision
of the "Lumpenproletarians" whom he had observed with
such intensity.

[3] From *The Orlov Couple,* written in 1897.

CHAPTER III

Wander Years

When Alexei Maximovich Peshkov signed his first published story *Maxim Gorky—Maxim the Bitter,* he took for himself the name he was to flaunt as a banner all the rest of his days. Thenceforth he was to be known to the world as M. Gorky or A. M. Gorky, but in civil matters he was still Alexei Maximovich Peshkov or A. M. Peshkov. It was the exceptional adversity of his childhood and the seamy side of life so closely observed in his young manhood that had made Alexei Maximovich choose the romantic pen name. But by the time he became a writer the bitter period of his existence was ending and, as a writer, his attitude toward life was troubled and compassionate, sometimes angry, but not bitter. In fact, Tolstoy once told the young writer, "It's quite remarkable that you should be so good-hearted when you have every reason to be bitter."[1]

The new "proletarian writer" was no more proletarian in origin than he was bitter in outlook, or an unlettered tramp. On both sides, parents and grandparents were lower middle class (*meshchane,* as he called them). His father, an upholsterer with a shop of his own, died of cholera when Alexei was not yet four. His mother's second marriage brought her a cruel, inconsiderate husband, and her boy Alexei a hateful

---

[1] M. Gorkii, *Vospominaniya o Lve Tolstom* (*Memories of Leo Tolstoy*) (Berlin, 1919). All quotations from or concerning Tolstoy in the present work are from these reminiscences. This work is Gorky's most brilliant literary study, for in it Tolstoy is observed as closely and portrayed as vividly as any of the *bosyaki*—barefoot ones—who were the heroes of his early tales. One may learn more about Tolstoy's spirit from these sketchy notes than from all the stout and learned studies of the great novelist.

stepfather. She and her son went to live with her parents. Galloping consumption carried off his mother when he was eleven, leaving him doubly orphaned at the home of his grandparents.

Nor did adversity end there. When he went to live with his grandfather, the fortunes of the latter had begun swiftly to decline, his small dye works being ruined by the growth of the new great dye factories. With the decline of his fortunes the old man became ill-tempered, miserly, cruel to his wife and his grandson. In the year of the death of the boy's mother, he hired young Alexei out as a shopboy in a shoestore. Followed misadventures as "apprentice" in various trades which he was never taught, as clerk, as cook's boy on a river steamer where his duties ranged from reading all sorts of books aloud to the cook to washing the galley dishes, as apprentice to an ikon painter, as helper in a cellar bakery, and many other transient occupations. He went on from hard master to hard master, and trade to trade, but completed none of his apprenticeships. What is important in that dreary, bitter period is that, having learned to read while still a child, he lived all the while another life filled with splendor, in a world of books and dreams.

His maternal grandfather had taught him Old Church Slavonic from the *Psalter* and the *Book of Hours;* his mother, current Russian. Though his formal schooling was nugatory, he had a wonderful and beloved teacher in his illiterate grandmother. From her lips he heard folk tales, lives of the saints, myths, legends, told with the natural poetry and simple credulity of a Russian woman of the people. His grandmother was the person he loved best. *Bogatyri,* saints, heroes, talking animals and birds, the Lord God and His Blessed Son, whom she confounded with each other and to whom she felt marvelously close and intimate, peopled the enchanted world she was never tired of revealing to the boy.

From her he got the sense of the poetry of life which runs through all the best of his prose, though when he tried to write verse it was always to be feeble and pallid.[2] From her he got his gift for storytelling, later enriched by reading other and more famous story tellers. A number of his tales are retellings of tales he heard from her. From her, too, he derived a warm and comforting religious feeling that caused him for a number of years to have a "romance with God" (the phrase is his own), and thereafter to enter on a lifelong quest for religious warmth in whatever faith he might hold, a habit that all of Lenin's angry chiding could never break.

The "bitter period" in young Alexei's life reached its climax at the tender age of eighteen, before his wander years began. The death of his grandmother at that same moment caused him to feel suddenly alone in an unfriendly world. He sought solace in the bashful courting of two girls at once; comparing notes with each other, both met him with amused rejection. Because of poverty and too-sketchy preparation, he was blocked in an attempt to start a higher education. These losses and frustrations, plus a bookish, "wordly-wise" pessimism derived from his reading, caused him to write the world an elegant farewell note, and aim a bullet at his heart.[3]

[2] In this judgment I am of course challenging all the critics of the Stalin era (for had not Joseph Stalin himself scrawled across the manuscript of the earliest of his poems, "The Maiden and Death": "This piece is greater than Goethe's Faust"?) and the judgment of Lenin as well, and indeed of the whole revolutionary generation of the early 1900s who thought of his *Pesnya o burevestnike* (Song of the Stormy Petrel) as the very pinnacle of poetry, although Gorky himself soon grew heartily sick of its hollow rhetoric and referred to it as "a mere fanciful invention" in his interview of 1928 on "How I Learned to Write." The *Kratkaya Literaturnaya Entsiklopedia* (Moscow, 1964) describes it not as a masterpiece of poetry but as a "revolutionary proclamation."

[3] The bookishness is attested by the note's text: "I beg that you hold responsible for my death the poet Heine who first invented *toothache of the heart* . . . and that my body be dissected to find out what sort of devil has been dwelling in me for the past few months."

He was acting out a role, but the bullet was real. Though it missed his heart, it damaged a lung, leaving a wound that was the source of the attacks of tuberculosis that plagued him at intervals for the rest of his life. Yet his constitution was fabulously strong. Within a month after the attempted suicide, he was back at his hard work in a bakery cellar; and, with the aid of occasional treatment and rest in a sunny clime, he lived out a long, stubborn, and active life, dying finally of tuberculosis, but not until the age of sixty-eight.

When the attempt to commit suicide ended in failure, the love of life surged up in him stronger than before. Now it was that he determined to wander, to see life, to know all Russia and the world of men. Up and down the Volga he ranged, deep into Central Russia, high into the mountains of the Caucasus, as far to the south as Bessarabia.

He dreamed besides of two other journeys: to Persia, which had possessed his imagination since he first laid eyes on a Persian merchant at a Nizhni Novgorod annual fair; and to a "true and just land, where people respect one another, and everything they do is decent and fine." These journeys he never made, but the first filled his reveries and the second made up the sum and substance of his "socialism."

From the experiences of his childhood, his succession of occupations, and his journeys among men and books, he was to write, "I accumulated such a load of impressions that I could not stop myself from writing." Those impressions were to be his stock in trade. In the fifth year of his wandering, all that was needed was the publication of a single tale and some advice from two experienced writers, and Alexei Maximovich Peshkov, Vagabond, became Maxim Gorky, Man of Letters.

Most of his best work was published during the next ten years: *Makar Chudra,* 1892; *Chelkash,* 1894; *The Old*

Woman Izergil (a portrayal of his grandmother and the re-telling of two of her folk tales), 1895; *The Orlov Couple,* 1897; *Twenty-Six Men and a Girl,* 1899; *Foma Gordeyev,* 1899; *The Lower Depths,* 1902.

If we add to these *The Confession,* 1908; *Strasti-mordasti,* 1913;[4] *Reminiscences of Leo Nikolaevich Tolstoy,* 1919; and his nostalgic autobiographical sketches that return to the same early material, it seems to me we have a fairly complete canon of the literary achievement of Maxim Gorky. The canon includes two of his novels *(Foma Gordeyev[5] and The Confession)*, and one of his plays *(The Lower Depths)*. Some might add one or two others of the early short tales, but no sensitive critic, unconstrained by Party dictation, would include his other plays, his poems, his didactic essays, the form-less, preachy novels of his late period, or the bulk of his political journalism written in Stalin's days. If these last are important, it is solely because they come from the pen of Maxim Gorky. The only political prose that might enter the company of his best work are his eloquent attacks on Lenin in *Revolyutsiya i Kultura* and his laudatory sketch of the same man written in 1924 under the impact of Lenin's death.

---

[4] The title is untranslatable.

[5] *Foma Gordeyev* differs from his other successful tales in that it deals not with Volga vagrants but Volga merchants. After his first triumphs Gorky was invited into the homes of merchant princes who admired this local writer as a self-made man like themselves. It is obvious from this novel that he admired them in turn. The Old Believer merchants, audacious founders of great mer-cantile-manufacturing empires, are pictured as men of creative imagination, strong-willed, far-sighted, free from restraining scruples, ardent lovers of power, builders of great enterprises, successful in all they undertake. It is only their children, born to wealth instead of creating and assembling it, who are pictured as incapable and foredoomed to failure and self-destruction.

CHAPTER IV

Liberty, Classes, Man, and God

During the years of his vagrant young manhood, Gorky seems to have developed all the basic ideas that were to inform his writing. These he would hold to stubbornly for the rest of his days; not even the *narodnik* Mihail Romas, who was his first mentor, nor the experienced writers to whom he apprenticed himself, Korolenko and Chekhov, nor any one of the strong-willed men to whom he attached himself in turn in his search for "a man with a true and living faith,"[1] was ever able substantially to alter them.

An examination of these basic ideas makes visible the abyss that separates Gorky from Lenin.

Love of Liberty. It was this that made the young Alexei Peshkov run away from his various employers to become a wanderer. It was the love of freedom in his vagabond heroes that caused him to romanticize their life. What he glorified in them was their freedom and strength, freedom from social and personal responsibility and from binding ties and pursuits and settled habitation, freedom to wander, strength to act on sudden impulses, even wild and lawless ones, and to defy "philistine and slavish" conventions. These free, strong, and undisciplined characters cannot for a moment be con-

---

[1] These fords come from Gorky's *Vospominaniya o Lve Nikolaeviche Tolstom* (Berlin, 1919) , but are applicable no less to the other "strong-willed men" to whom Gorky attached himself: "I kept studying Tolstoy so intensely because I was seeking then, am still seeking now, and shall continue to seek until I die for a man with a true and living faith." *Ibid.*, p. 49 The date of publication of these words is 1919, while Gorky was working closely with Lenin in an effort to salvage Russian culture and save the lives of Russian intellectuals. (On this, see Chapters VII, VIII and IX.)

founded with Lenin's factory-disciplined workingmen, nor
with his "professional revolutionaries" drilled in the military discipline of a conspirative army. Rather do they represent, as Alexei Tolstoy was shrewdly to note, "Gorky's ideal
of a *bosyak,* intellectuals dressed up in romantic dirty
rags."

Several times, under the pressure of the milieu into which
he entered as a successful writer, Gorky tried to portray a
class-conscious militant proletarian. Always the result was
lifeless and cold. Yet he had no trouble portraying khans,
princes, merchants, legendary heroes, or Promethean figures
of legend like the Danko of his grandmother's tale of the
man of vision who tried to lead men out of a dark swampy
forest into a bright clear land, and who, when their courage
and faith in him faltered in the darkness, snatched his own
burning heart out of his breast to light up their path.[2]

For a few years, the young Gorky earned his living as a
newspaper columnist. His columns make dull reading, yet

[2] The continuity of Gorky's ideas and even his images is shown by comparing his characterization of the merchant prince Gordeyev (1899) , the Promethean folk hero of his grandmother's tale Danko (1895) , and his characteriza-
tions of Lenin of 1918, 1920 and 1924.

The merchant princes of the Volga, Ignat Gordeyev and his associates, have
Lenin's concentration on power, his insistence on a wide network of organization which must embrace everybody and everything and put each man in his
proper place, even Lenin's monolithic dream that "When the state is able to
inspire all its citizens with a single opinion, compelling everyone to think
alike, that is beauty," words quoted from one of Gorky's merchant princes,
not from Lenin. Of Ignat Gordeyev he wrote: "He was one of those people
who are always and in everything accompanied by success—not merely
because they are talented and fond of hard work, but more because, possessing
enormous reserves of energy, as they make their way they do not ponder, in
fact are incapable of pondering over their choice of means. . . ." These
sentences from the novel *Foma Gordeyev* were written in 1898 and 1899,
before he knew Lenin. They appear almost verbatim in his hostile characteri-
zations of Lenin in 1918 and in his hagiographical memoir of 1924.

In the 1924 memoir, Danko reappears too: "For me Lenin is a hero of
legend, the man who tears out of his own breast his burning heart in order by
its fire to light up for people the road out of the shameful chaos of our time,
out of the rotting and bloody swamp of stifling 'statism.' "

when he writes of freedom there is sometimes a spark of fire. Thus in the *Nizhegorodskii Listok* of March 31, 1901:

Are there among you real men? Perhaps five out of a thousand are such as believe passionately that man is a creator and master of life, and that his right to think and speak in freedom is a sacred right. Perhaps five out of a thousand fight for that right and are ready fearlessly to perish in the struggle for it. But the majority of you are either the slaves of life or its impudent masters—timid philistines temporarily taking the place of real men.

"The right to think in freedom and to speak in freedom" was in Gorky's mind first of all a right for men of letters, men of the written and spoken word, a right he claimed just as resoundingly under Lenin's dictatorship as he had under the Tsar's autocracy. To Andreev, Gorky wrote in 1902:

A Russian writer should never live in friendship with the Russian government. It doesn't matter what kind it may be: autocratic, constitutional, or—even!—republican. . . . In all three forms our [government] will by its very essence be equally trashy.[3]

Contrary to official legend, he was a consistent opponent of party control of literature, detesting the idea that party or government bureaucracy—or officious critics—should tell a writer what to write. He welcomed suggestions from experienced writers concerning his craft, but when advice became peremptory or prescriptive, he felt "hatred of those critics who imagine themselves to be district supervisors in the literary section, and, like all Russian policemen, have lost their respect for individuality and individual freedom."[4]

[3] Peter Yershov, ed. *Letters of M. Gorky and L. Andreev, 1899–1912* (New York, 1958), p. 41.
[4] *Ibid.*, p. 104.

Gorky's stories were full of anger at life. But his anger and his fellow feeling for his characters were something quite distinct from the prevailing "social protest" that ignored the deeper roots of tragedy in the nature of man and of life itself and sought to explain all evil as a mere by-product of the legal forms of ownership, destined to disappear once these forms were transformed.

As a provincial writer in Nizhni Novgorod, Gorky had organized charities and provided sleigh rides, warm boots, skates, and other gifts for children, medicines, food, outings, festivals. As one Bolshevik wrote to Lenin at the time, "Maxim Gorky now spends less than thirty percent of his earnings on himself."

In the early 1900s the revolutionary political parties acquired sufficient influence over him to divert much of his already large earnings, and of the far larger sums he collected from the wealthy, away from his charities and into help for the revolutionary movement. But he never gave up his habit of showing private generosity and charity to persons "deserving" and "undeserving," and he stubbornly resisted attempts to enlist him as an exclusive contributor to a single party or faction. He gave freely to all, to anarchists, Social Revolutionaries, Mensheviks, Bolsheviks, revolutionary democrats, and liberals. Gorky has told us he got Savva Morozov to contribute 2,000 rubles a month to Lenin's "finance minister," Leonid Krassin. Lenin never thought to ask how "class interest" could induce Morozov, Schmidt, Bugrov, and other millionaires to contribute to his fighting funds to be used to destroy their class. For the answer to this question he could have gotten little help from Marx, but perhaps some from Sigmund Freud, who would have called it *the death wish*.[5]

---

[5] In 1918, when *Pravda* attacked Gorky's *Novaya Zhizn* as being "financed by the bourgeoisie," Gorky answered with a personal accounting, then added: "From 1901 to 1917, hundreds of thousands of rubles passed through

The political-minded critics of the early 1900's wanted more than money from the "proletarian novelist," pressing him to engage in political activity. He drew up or signed a few protests, wrote nonpolitical tales for literary sections of political journals, suffered some police persecution which deepened his hatred of autocracy, but resisted the pressure to do political-thesis narratives. In 1902 he made one such attempt, a play called *Meshchane* (variously translated as *The Middle Class, The Philistines, Smug Citizens*). The result makes dismal reading, and Gorky was sufficiently self-critical to realize it. To Chekhov he wrote: "Well, the play has turned out to be clamorous, beastly, empty and dull. I dislike it greatly. . . . This very winter I will without fail write another play. . . . This one will have to be finely proportioned and beautiful as music."

For this second play he returned to the people and the life he knew so well. *Na Dne* (*At the Bottom, The Lower Depths, Lodging for a Night*) is indeed a play with the thematic structure of a musical composition.[6]

Again in 1907, Gorky tried his hand at a propaganda work in the novel *Mother,* celebrated beyond its merits because Lenin found it most "useful to the party" and hence the most valuable of Gorky's writings. He wrote it not on order from Lenin's party but out of loneliness and impotent vexation as the Tsar's government reestablished itself after the ebbing of the storm of 1905–1906 and he was forced to leave his native land.

---

my hands for the cause of the Social Democratic Party. Less than ten thousand came from me personally, the major portion from the 'bourgeoisie.' *Iskra* was published with the money of Savva Morozov. . . . Your filthy sallies against *Novaya Zhizn* disgrace not my journal but yourselves."

[6] Lenin, Krupskaya tells us cryptically, "saw Gorky's *Lower Depths* at the [Moscow] Art Theater in 1922 . . . but he disliked the theatricality of the production, the absence of those details of social life which . . . portray the environment in all its concreteness."

If a tooth could feel after being knocked out [he wrote] it would probably feel as lonely as I. . . . Everything lost . . . they had crushed, annihilated, exiled, imprisoned everybody. . . . I felt as if a pestilential dust were blowing from Russia.

On Lenin's say-so, Soviet critics treat *Mother* as "the first proletarian novel" and the progenitor of the grim school of "socialist realism." After he read it, Lenin sought a private encounter with Gorky to persuade him to accept the idea of *partiinost* (party spirit) and to limit both his financial and his literary contributions exclusively to Lenin's own faction. Gorky helped the Bolshevik leader generously but refused to yield to the demand for factional exclusiveness. In *Novaya Zhizn* in 1917 he could still write:

For seventeen years I have considered myself a Social Democrat and have served as well as I could the purposes of that Party. But I have never denied my services to other parties, for I am unwilling to spurn any vital cause. I have no sympathy for people who become fossilized and petrified under the pressure of the faith they confess. I go further: In every party and group I regard myself as a heretic. In my political views there are quite likely a number of contradictions which I cannot and do not want to reconcile with each other. . . . I should have to kill utterly that part of my soul which loves most passionately the aching, live, sinful, and—if you please—wretchedly pitiful Russian man.

One of Gorky's oldest friends, Ekaterina Kuskova, in her memoir on the writer composed under the impact of his death, gave us an admirable picture of his "Marxism" and the ambivalence of his admiration for Lenin. In 1893, when Maxim Gorky had just published his first book of tales, Kuskova took the young man, so hungry to "learn everything," into her home, well-stocked with books, and into the circle of Nizhni Novgorod intellectuals. The learned woman and the ardent tramp writer found they had much in common. Both were from the Volga, born in Kazan and living in

Nizhni; both loved books and revered learning. She guided his reading, suggesting subjects and titles and helping him to understand what he read. But in one thing she was unsuccessful: admirer of Marx though she was, she could not persuade him to take Marx's *Capital*. Many years later, when she learned of his new-found admiration for Lenin, she asked him:

What has brought you to the Bolsheviks? Do you remember how I began to read Marx with you in Nizhni, and you proposed to throw the "German philistine" into the fire and go out to the garden wall to listen, free from bookishness, to the singing of the nightingale . . . ?

Oh, he cried out, smiling—"Now, too, I prefer nightingales to Marxist rubbish. I can't take it, by God, even on an empty stomach. But . . . as people they are excellent. Most excellent people, I tell you. They will knock the autocracy's head off, just like that. . . . Excellent people. . . . And Lenin, by God, sings like a nightingale. . . ."

I looked at him. In his eyes were sparks of laughter. Is he mocking? Or has he been taken in somehow? In any case, after this moment of attraction as before, he continued warmly to support every other "activism" aiming at "smashing the ugly mug" of the autocracy. . . .

And, after October [1917], when these "most excellent people" were victorious, nobody attacked them with such definite sharpness as Gorky, whose ideal of "man" suffered from the "usurpers of freedom."[7]

As with so much in Soviet historiography, there are different and contradictory versions of the date and nature of Gorky's first face-to-face meeting with Lenin. At least as early as 1903, when there was a great to-do about Lenin's splitting of the *Iskra* group and the Second Party Congress into Bol-

[7] E. Kuskova, "Na rubezhe dvukh epokh: Pamyati A. M. Gorkogo" (On the Border Between Two Epochs: In Memory of A. M. Gorky), *Posledniya Novosti* (Paris), June 26, 1936.

sheviks and Mensheviks, his name must have been well known to Maxim Gorky. Given Gorky's interest and keen powers of observation, he would undoubtedly have made precise mental notes on this strong-willed man whenever he met him for the first time, as he did on all the other "strong" characters he had observed from tramps to Tolstoy. If we are to trust Gorky's always vivid powers of observation, and the express words of his remarkable description of Vladimir Ilyich in his *Days with Lenin,* the two did not meet until the London Congress of the Social Democratic Party in 1907.

> I had never met Lenin before this [Gorky writes]. I did not expect Lenin to be like that. There was something lacking in him. . . . He was somehow too ordinary, did not give the impression of being a leader. As a literary man I am obliged to take note of such details. . . .[8]

It is such "little details" that make Gorky's literary profiles so vivid, whether he is dealing with a tramp or with Lenin or Tolstoy.

In 1934, however, when Stalin's great "Operation Rewrite" was in high gear, one of its objectives was to enlarge the role of Lenin in the revolution of 1905. As early as 1931, Stalin attacked an honest writer on an obscure problem of Party history, namely the date on which Lenin first lost his admiration for Kautsky. In an ominous letter to *Proletarskaya Revolyutsiya* Stalin charged its editors with "rotten liberalism" for having printed the historian's findings, though they had cautiously labeled the study a "discussion article." The historian disappeared, and "rotten liberalism," "bourgeois objectivism," and "exaggerated attachment to facts," as well as various "archive rats," disappeared with him. Immediately pliant memorialists appeared, ready to

---

[8] Gorky, *Days with Lenin,* (New York: International Publishers [i.e., the official Comintern version], 1932), pp. 4–5.

"remember" whatever "past" Stalin wished to have remembered.[9]

Among these memorialists was K. P. Pyatnitsky, one-time business manager of Gorky's publishing house, Znanie, who now "remembered" that Lenin had planned the Moscow uprising of December 1905 from an apartment in St. Petersburg, and that Gorky had gone from Moscow to St. Petersburg on November 16, 1905, "to report to Lenin on the mood of the Moscow workingmen." Thereupon, the Stalinist historian Sorin, head of the Lenin Section of the Marx-Engels-Lenin Institute, wrote Gorky asking him to confirm this meeting and his report to Lenin in 1905. The author of *Days with Lenin* was living in Stalin's Russia in 1934, when histories were succeeding each other as if they were being consumed by a giant chain smoker who lights the first volume of the new work with the last volume of the old, and historians were appearing and disappearing . . . and vanishing without a trace.

Gorky did the best he could, explaining uncomfortably that he must have gone to report to Lenin "with a high fever, as the result of which my memory of what took place was so confused that I even did not make up my mind to say anything about it in my memories of Vl. Ilyich." And Gorky's second wife, the actress Andreeva, obligingly remembered how long the two men had held each other's hands in their first handclasp, how joyously they had smiled into each other's faces, and how Gorky could not get over the pleasure of the meeting for many hours, but she says nothing about a

[9] For an analysis of this phenomenon see the writer's "Operation Rewrite: The Agony of the Soviet Historian," *Foreign Affairs*, October 1952, reprinted in Bertram Wolfe, *Communist Totalitarianism* (Boston, 1961); and my paper presented at a historiography symposium in Geneva under the auspices of the Institut Universitaire des Hautes Études Internationales in 1961, reprinted in John Keep and Liliana Brisby, eds., *Contemporary History in the Soviet Mirror* (London, 1964). The paper is entitled "Party Histories from Lenin to Khrushchev."

deliberate journey to meet Lenin nor about a "report on the mood of the Moscow workingmen."[10]

Whether we are to accept the idea that a high fever in 1905 confused Gorky into saying that "I met Lenin for the first time in London in 1907," or that the first meeting and "report" were so casual that Lenin made no impression upon him, or, as seems most likely, that no meeting between them took place in 1905, the fact remains that Gorky's first awareness of Lenin as a human being whom he was meeting face to face and observing with enormous interest and with his remarkable writer's attention to life-giving details, was the result of an invitation to attend the London Party Congress of 1907 as an "honorary guest."

Lenin had just finished the novel *Mother*. After reading it, he introduced into the Central Committee, then consisting of both Mensheviks and Bolsheviks, a motion to invite Gorky to the London Congress. The motion was adopted unanimously. No sooner had Gorky registered at a London hotel than Lenin called on him to make his acquaintance. Barely stopping to shake hands, Vladimir Ilyich rushed past his host to the bed in the middle of the room, thrust his hand into the bedclothes, and began moving it around between the sheets.

I stood like a dolt [Gorky told Valentinov afterward] unable to understand what he was up to. Had he lost his mind! But praise be to Allah, my bewilderment ceased when he returned to my side and explained: "In London the climate is raw and we must see to it that the bedding isn't damp. And," says he, "we must be particularly careful in your case since you have just written *Mother*, a thing useful for the Russian workingman which sum-

[10] See *Chronicle*, Vol. IV, p. 386; *V. I. Lenin i Maksim Gorkii*, pp. 291, 423; *V. I. Lenin o Literature i Iskusstve* (V. I. Lenin on Literature and Art), (Moscow, 1957), 568, 575–76. This last work, strangely, dates Gorky's letter to Sorin in the Marx-Engels-Lenin Institute as June 12, 1928, while the *Chronicle* and the volume on *V. I. Lenin and Maxim Gorky* put the exchange of letters correctly in 1934.

mons him to battle against the autocracy." Of course, I thanked him for his compliment, but I must admit I was a bit annoyed. . . . To treat my work as if it were a kind of committee manifesto calling for the storming of the autocracy . . . was after all quite unfitting. You see, in this work I tried to treat some very large and very, very difficult problems. The justifying of terror, assassination, and executions during a revolution—you see, that's a big moral problem. You see, it's not possible so lightly to get around the thought that perhaps such killings sully a sacred cause.[11]

Gorky's artistic instincts told him that *Mother* was a poor work. When a Soviet theater manager wanted to have it dramatized in the early twenties, he refused consent, yielding only when the director touched his heart by the promise that half the proceeds would be given to the *besprizornyi*, waifs made fatherless and homeless by the ravages of war and famine. In 1927, when Gladkov wrote apologetically that he found *Mother* artistically weak and dull and was unable to finish it, Gorky replied, "You are wrong to think that your critical—and quite just—attitude toward *Mother* might offend me. . . . *Mother* is a really bad book, written under the spell of bad temper and irritation after the events of 1906. . . ."

In 1932 when Bertold Brecht attempted a dramatization of Gorky's *Mother* he reduced it to a bare propaganda piece, treating it as if it were "a committee manifesto" dramatized. The Russian background, the moral complexity, the "large and difficult problems" in Gorky's novel, all disappeared, and Bertold Brecht's usually unerring sense of theater deserted him. Thus did the artist's appraisal of his own novel prove sounder than the politician's.

Three years before his death, Gorky pronounced his final judgment on the work to his biographer and friend, V. A.

[11] N. Valentinov, "Vstrechi s M. Gorkim" (Meetings with M. Gorky), *Novyi Zhurnal*, (New York), No. 78, 1965, pp. 138–39.

Desnitsky: *"Mother* [he wrote] is long drawn-out, boringly and carelessly written."[12]

On the subject of party orders and freedom for the writer, we can give the last word to an utterance of Gorky to Konstantin Fedin, which the latter did not dare include in his *Gorky in Our Midst* written during the Stalin era, but repeated privately to Victor Serge: "The party commissar is at one and the same time policeman, censor, and archbishop: he grabs hold of you, blue-pencils your writings, and then wants to sink his claws into your soul."[13]

Worker and Peasant. Gorky's "congenital disgust with politics" Lenin could forgive in an artist, but not his infuriating refusal to rule out opposition Bolsheviks, Mensheviks, anarchists, Social Revolutionaries as unworthy of support. Nor could he overlook the fact that Gorky could never bring himself to accept Lenin's simplistic division of men into classes or his condemnation of whole categories of men to extermination.

Only the peasants he sometimes treated as an impersonal

[12] For the exchange of letters with Gladkov, see *Literaturnoe Nasledstvo* (Moscow, 1963), Vol. XVII, pp. 63, 95. For his opposition to the dramatization of the novel, *Ibid.*, p. 230, letter 6 and note 1. His letter to Desnitsky is cited by David Shub, "Maksim Gorkii i Kommunistichicheskaya Diktatura," *Mosty* (Munich), No. 1, 1958, p. 249. For Bercht's version, see Brecht, *Die Mutter, nach Gorky* (Berlin, 1933). For quotations from the unfavorable newspaper reviews of January 18, 1932, see Brecht's own citations from the reviews, and his answers thereto on pages 70–74 of the same work. To make matters worse, even the Soviet press treated Brecht's dramatization unfavorably.

[13] Victor Serge, "Recollections of Maxim Gorky" in *Pages from the Diary of Victor Serge* cited in the *New International* (New York), July–August 1950, p. 249. Fedin was writing in the bleakest period of Stalin's rule so that Gorky's words on freedom from party censorship is not the only omission. There is nothing about Gorky's attempt to save the life of the poet Gumilev, nothing on Trotsky, nothing on Gorky's protest at the suppression of the Kronstadt sailors, nothing on Gorky's opposition to the Red Terror, nothing on Boris Pilniak, whose life Gorky saved. And there are other eloquent silences.

category, for he had seen and experienced so many bitter things among peasants. At twenty he watched his first intellectual mentor and then employer, the Narodnik Mikhail Romas, found a general store in the village of Krasnovidovo, where he hoped the peasants might gather of a winter evening around the stove, buy goods at low prices, and fill their heads gratis with noble ideas. But incited by village notables and their own hostility to incomprehensible alien ways, the peasants were suspicious of these outsiders. Gunpowder was put into the stove, both he and his employer were ambushed at night, finally the store was burned down and they had to flee for their lives into the flickering darkness before a pursuing band. Then at twenty-three he had been beaten into unconsciousness when he tried to save a naked woman who was being horsewhipped publicly through a village street by her husband and followed by a howling mob, because she had been taken in adultery. These experiences of his young manhood made him fear the peasant and hate him.

In 1922, in his *O Russkom Krestyanstve,* he sought to rationalize this hatred. Lumping peasants then with the workers of the cities, whom he sometimes grudgingly idealized but more often regarded with gloomy clarity, he wrote:

In its essence every people is spontaneously anarchic; the folk wants as far as possible to eat more and work less, have all rights and no duties. The atmosphere of rightlessness in which . . . the folk is accustomed to live convinces it of the lawfulness of lawlessness, the zoological naturalness of anarchism. . . . The Russian peasant has been dreaming for centuries of some sort of state without any right to influence his personal will or his liberty of action—a state with no power over man.

He was ready to recognize the peasant's love for the land as a "mystic love," and quoted a fine old bearded muzhik as saying to him:

Yes, we have learned to fly like sparrows, and to swim like sardines, but we don't know how to live on earth. We must first settle well on earth and let the air come afterwards. . . . If we peasants had made the revolution ourselves everything would long ago be quiet on earth and orderly. The peasant knows how to work—only give him land. He doesn't organize strikes—the earth won't let him. . . .

After citing such peasants with approval, Gorky returns to his ineluctable fear:

Cruelty—that is what has tormented me all my life and torments me now. . . . In Russian cruelty one finds a diabolical refinement, something subtle and cultivated. . . . This inventive cruelty was influenced by the reading of the lives of the martyred and tortured saints. . . .

Follows an account of well-nigh unprintable tortures he had witnessed during the Civil War. One of the gentler examples will suffice:

Undressing an officer naked, they tore bits of skin in the shape of epaulettes from his shoulders, and in place of the little stars hammered in nails; they cut strips of skin along the line of the trouser stripes and sword belt—this they called "dressing him up in a uniform." It took no little time and considerable art. . . .
Who was the crueler: the Whites or the Reds? Probably they were both alike. You see, both one side and the other—were Russians. . . .

Gorky was convinced that Lenin's seizure of power and his demagogic calls for terror from below would give free rein to peasant cruelty until it wiped out the cities which to him were the focus of culture and humaneness. In the end this judgment was to prove wrong, for it was from the city that the more ferocious forms of cruelty (forced collectivization, millions of families at slave labor, the great blood purges,

inquisitorial torture to fabricate "confessions," the regimen-
tation and atomization of society and of the intellect) were
to come. Yet there can be no doubt it was this justified if
one-sided hatred and fear of the peasants that caused Gorky
to misread for a time the brutal meaning of forced collectivization and to accept momentarily the massive concentration
camps and forced labor armies, semantically disguised as
"re-education centers," under Joseph Stalin.[14]

On the subject of the workingman, Gorky's mind was a
whirlpool driven round and round by the conflicting forces
of his own clear-eyed observation and the idealizing indoctri-
nation to which he was subjected by the socialist intellectual
milieu that accepted him as the celebrator of the lives of the
men of the lower depths. Both in his letters and in *Na Dne*,
he expressed dislike of the habit of certain "class-conscious
workingmen" who boast, "I'm a worker," much as a member
of the gentry boasts, "I'm a nobleman." In *The Lower
Depths*, Gorky has Peppel, the thief, quote the locksmith,
Kletsch, in ironic tones:

> "I am a workingman" [he says]—and everybody's below him,
> he'll have you believe. Well, work if you like it—what's there to
> be proud of? If we're supposed to judge people by their work,
> then the horse is better than any man—you drive it—and it
> doesn't talk back.

At other times Gorky expressed the hope that the workingman, as a city dweller, would not prove insensitive to the
enlightenment offered by the intellectual, and that he might
be illumined by the light of culture, science, "Europe" (by
which Gorky means European civilization), and joy in heroic and creative work. Sometimes, as in the Stalin years, he
tried to persuade himself that the worker was actually rejoic-

[14] Gorky said of the peasant writer Podyachev: "Thanks to him we now
have a better idea of the beast in the shape of a man that lives in the Russian
village." Valentinov, *op. cit.,* p. 132.

ing at the speedup and privations of forced industrialization and had become an ancient Russian *bogatyr,* a titan engaged in heroic, legendary feats of labor. But the illusion did not last. The whirlpool made a turn and he saw the workingman as yesterday's peasant, with the same limited horizon, anarchic cruelty and laziness, with not even a redeeming attachment to his work to match the peasant's mystic attachment to his piece of land. What if on getting power, he asks, the worker should repeat the age-old saying, "All one needs is a quiet corner and a woman"?

What if indeed the millions of Russia suffer the bitter pains of the revolution only because in the depths of their souls they cherish the hope of liberation from work? A minimum of labor and a maximum of satisfaction—that is quite as unobtainable as any other [utopia].

Knowing well this whirlpool in his own mind, Gorky wrote in his memoir on Lenin at the latter's death, "I am a very dubious Marxist. . . . I do not have any faith in the intelligence of the masses in general."

Man, the Creator of Life. In the main, Gorky's writings deal not with classes but with man. The very word *man* stirred such feeling in him that, as we have seen, he found it difficult to write it without a capital. At the very outset of his career he voiced the hope that what he wrote might express "eternal truths" with "imperishable beauty," so that his work might live and serve man. In a dialogue between Writer and Reader (1898), the Writer declares that the aim of his art is to "help man understand himself, raise his faith in himself, wage war against vulgarity in men, arouse in their minds shame, wrath, courage . . . make them noble and strong, make them capable of suffusing their life with the holy spirit of beauty."

It is a confession of faith. But a sense of the difficulty of this high resolve makes him give to the Reader in that dialogue the last word, a mocking word concerning the blind leading the blind, and a troubling question—one that was to trouble Maxim Gorky always: "How can you be a guide when you yourself do not know the road?"

To Andreev, Gorky wrote in 1905:

You see, man stands between two bottomless pits, birth and death. . . . He knows that the earth one fine day may fall into the sun and turn into steam, along with him, libraries, museums, babies, valuables—along with all the material and spiritual work of many centuries, along with everything dear to him, everything he loves. Now look at him from this tragic aspect . . . and then you'll see that, although he knows of the future ruin, ruin without a trace, of all the work of his muscles and his spirit, he keeps on working, keeps on creating . . . not to put off this ruin but simply from some sort of proud stubbornness. "Yes, I'll perish, and perish without a trace, but first I'll build temples, and I'll create great works. Yes, I know that they too will perish without a trace, but I'll create them just the same, since I want to!" That's the human voice. And believe me, a real man who is truly free always values his human worth, and is always conscious of mortality—both of himself and of all that surrounds him.

And to Tolstoy, when the two were convalescing in the Crimea, Gorky said:

Even a great book is no more than a dead, dark shadow of the Word. It only hints at the Truth, whereas man is a depository of the living God. . . . I deeply believe that there is nothing better on earth than man. Only man exists, the rest is no more than a point of view. . . . I have always been a Man-worshipper, only I have not been able to express it with sufficient force.

Two major motifs are interwoven in the play *Na Dne*. One is this theme of Man, with a capital M. The cunning old wanderer, Luka, Gorky's principal mouthpiece, rings the changes of the theme, now echoed, now called in question, by each of the other characters in turn. Luka has no sooner entered the "cavelike basement" than he rebukes the declassed Baron for taking pride in his vanished estate. "All of you are just human beings. Put on as much as you like, wriggle as much as you will, but just as you are born a man, a man you will die." By way of counterpoint, he assures the broken-down Actor: "Man can do everything . . . if he only wants to."

To each of these creatures that once were men, the pilgrim Luka gives sympathy, instills courage, encourages a forlorn hope "to live better"—or at least to die more easily.

When the other lodgers, long used to the failing health of the dying Anna, speak mockingly of imaginary attendants waiting on her, the old wanderer comforts her in her last hours, and rebukes the callous fellow inmates of the cellar:

How can anybody make a joke of it? How can anybody cast off a human being . . . ? Whatever condition he may be in, he is always worth something. There'll be peace and quiet there [he assures her]. . . . Death quiets everything. Death is kind to us humans. When you die, you'll have rest . . . for where can a human being find rest in this world? . . . You have to die with joy, without fear. To us, I tell you, death is like a mother to little children.

Only to the brutal lodging-house owner, Kostylov, does Luka deny manhood, telling him in riddles that "some people are mere people while others are truly men." Dispossessed for his defense of Kostylov's victims from the cellarlord's wrath and brutality, Luka resumes his wandering. The last act seems the poorer for his absence, yet, one by one, the other characters take up his theme of the meaningfulness of man, arguing its truth or falsity, its sense or nonsense, developing it further, until at last the character Satín, who in

some ways is Luka's antagonist, assumes the old man's defense in a drunken eulogy from which swell the triumphant
notes of the old man's theme:

What's truth? *Man*—that's the truth! He understood this—you
don't. . . . I can't get the old man out of my head. . . . The old
man had a head on his shoulders. . . . He had the same effect on
me as acid on an old dirty coin. . . . Everybody [he said], everybody lives for something better. That's why we have to be considerate of every man—Who knows what's in him, why he was
born, and what he can do? Maybe he was born . . . for our
greater good. . . . A man is free—he pays for everything himself—for belief and disbelief, for love, for intelligence, and that
makes him free. Man—that's the truth. What is man? It's not
you, nor I, nor they—No it's you, I, and they . . . all in one. You
understand? It's tremendous! In this are all the beginnings and
all the ends. Everything in man, everything for man. Only man
exists, the rest is the work of his hands and brain. Man! that is
splendid! It has a proud sound! . . .

Tolstoy said to Gorky concerning *Na Dne*, "Much of what
you say comes out of yourself, and therefore you have no
characters, and all your people have the same face." This is
true. It deprives *Na Dne* of ordinary theatricality but gives it
its poetic or, as Gorky put it, its symphonic development. For
this reason the traditional Moscow Art Theater treatment of
the play as a realistic drama of life in the lower depths—the
endless hours spent by actors and directors slumming in dens
and hovels, studying drunkards, vagabonds and prostitutes,
the meticulous attention to such matters as to how to roll a
makhorka cigarette—got the play off to a wrong start. It
became tremendously popular as a supposed drama of social
protest concerning "a society that compels men to live in
such misery," and as such it made Gorky's reputation in
many lands.

But as one reads it, or sees it performed in another tradi-

tion, one becomes aware that *Na Dne* is more than a realistic
picture of men at the bottom—more, and quite different. It
is Gorky's confession of faith. Its characters do not speak in
language appropriate to their lives and their diminished
estate. It is a liturgical-poetic drama filled with Gorky's
anger and despair at the way life is; Gorky's hope-
against-hope for man and what he may become; Gorky's
faltering doubt that this, his dream, can be fulfilled. At the
bottom of life as at its every level, he is saying, man is man,
with the same hopes, dreams, passions, weaknesses, illusions,
the same hopeless condition, the same potentialities for hope.
The play is what Gorky told Chekhov it would be, a tone
poem in dramatic form, with derelict men and women as the
orchestral instruments taking up, developing and interweaving its two themes. The first of these themes is Man. The
second we must reserve for consideration in the next chapter.
It is as an interweaving of two themes in a poetic drama that
the play must be read, and as poetry it must be played.
Indeed, it is the only completely successful poem Gorky ever
wrote.

In Quest of God. In 1901, Gorky and Tolstoy talked about
God:

"The minority feel the need of God [Gorky records Tolstoy as
saying] because they already have everything else, and the majority because they have nothing." But I would put it differently:
The majority believe in God out of weakness of spirit, and only a
few out of fullness of soul.[15]

This is authentic Gorky and authentic Tolstoy. It infuri-
ated Lenin when he discovered this mystic streak in his "first
proletarian novelist." Even in the novel *Mother* this should
have been visible to Lenin, had he not chosen to overlook it.
The hero, Pavel, permits himself to be persuaded by the

[15] Gorky, *Vospominaniya o Lve Nikolaeviche Tolstom*, p. 11.

peasant, Rybin, that "God exists in the reason of man, though not in the Church." The problem propounded by the novel, "whether terror, assassinations and executions do not sully a sacred cause," is a moral and religious one. And Pavel's mother becomes reconciled to her son's consorting with revolutionaries only after she has managed to identify them with the Christian martyrs of her faith. "Errors," Lenin thought, "but I shall explain them when we meet." And so he did, while Gorky, seeming not to hear, made no reply. Within a year, they were on the outs again—because of God!

In the author's unhappy days as an orphan, one of his few consoling joys had been the religion into which his beloved grandmother drew him. Religion gave him his first letters in the form of Old Church Slavonic; its sonorous phrases crept into his writing and colored his thought. Music, incense, tapers, ikons, church services, the simple, vivid language in which his grandmother talked to God, formed a corner of light and warmth in his cold and wretched childhood. "During those days [Gorky wrote] my thoughts and feelings relating to God formed the principal nourishment of my soul, the most beautiful things that life gave me. God was the best, the brightest of my surroundings, God and my grandmother, so friendly with all creatures."

Later, when learned men and books had shaken his faith, he felt that virtue had gone out of him. As late as 1919, as we have seen, when he was writing of Tolstoy, he said: "I was seeking then, I am still seeking now, and shall continue to seek until I die, for a man with a true and living faith."[16] This quest for a living faith brought him to Lenin as it had

---

[16] In the same work Gorky records that Tolstoy inspired in him the feeling, "I am not an orphan on the earth so long as this man lives on it." And the *Memories* end with the words, "And I, who do not believe in God, cast a stealthy, almost timid glance at him and said to myself: 'This man is like God.'"

to Tolstoy, but it was a quest which, as Gorky formulated it, aroused Lenin to fits of uncontrollable rage.

In 1906, Gorky wrote a book about an orphan, *The Story of a Man Nobody Needed,* a *roman policier* whose miserable central character is too weak to resist evil, becomes a police spy, and ends by committing suicide.

A dialogue between the orphan protagonist and his uncle, the village blacksmith, marks the beginning of a new stage in Gorky's search:

> "Why does God let devils into the church?"
> "What's it to him? God isn't the church watchman."
> "Doesn't he live there?"
> "God? What for? His place is everywhere. Churches are for people."
> "But what are people for?"
> "But people—they, so to speak . . . in general, for everything! Without people you can't manage anything—isn't that so . . . ?"
> "They—are they for God?"
> The smith looked sideways at his nephew and answered hesitatingly: "Of course. . . ."[17]

The wretched orphan of the novel, Yevsei, is Alexei Maximovich transposed; there, he might say, but for the grace of God, go I. But the voice of the blacksmith is Gorky's, too, hesitating to decide whether God is for the people, or the people for God. With this question, the quest is renewed.

Later that same year the *Mercure de France* conducted an international *enquête* concerning religion. Gorky answered that he opposed the religions of Moses, Christ, and Mahomet because they engendered antagonisms among men and subordinated them to outside forces. He offered instead a religious faith in man, not in man as he was but as he might

---

[17] M. Gorkii *Sobranie, Sochinenii* (Moscow, 1961), Vol. V, *Zhizn Nenuzhnogo Cheloveka* (*The Story of a Man Nobody Needed*), p. 11.

become if he strove to make himself into a "perfect being" through the development of all his faculties and "a happy and proud awareness of a harmonious link that joins him to the universe."[18]

At the end of 1907 Gorky began work on a new novel, *Ispoved* (*The Confession*), destined to take its place alongside *Na Dne* as a confession of faith. It is a narrative poem in biblical and liturgical prose. It has fared ill with Russian critics because of its very virtues, which to them seem to be its vices. Before Lenin knew what the work was about, he asked the author for an excerpt to publish in the literary section of *Proletarii*, but when he read the piece, he returned it with a curt demand that it be revised, or something else be sent in its place. With this ultimatum the friendship between the two men cooled for several years.

Gorky's *Ispoved* is more than a confession of faith; it is as well a statement of the proposition that the socialist movement is a surrogate religious creed.[19] The hero of the novel again is an orphan, this time called Matvei, who like Alexei Peshkov—Gorky himself—wanders through the world in quest of a "true and living faith." He visits monasteries, talks with holy men, joins pilgrimages, seeks wisdom from a celebrated and prideful religious man who indulges in coarse talk about women (modeled on Tolstoy). In the end, he gets

[18] *Mercure de France*, April 15, 1907 (April 2, Old Style); reproduced in Russian in *Nov*, April 5, O.S., 1907. Soviet works about Gorky in Russian tend to be silent about this interview, as if it were a shameful thing. Neither in *V. I. Lenin i A. M. Gorkii, Pisma, vospominaniya, dokumenty*, published jointly in 1958 by the Marxism Leninism Institute of the C.C.C.P.S.U. and the Gorky Institute of World Literature of the Academy of Sciences, nor in the enlarged German version published in East Berlin in 1964 is there any mention of it. The four-volume *Chronicle* (Vol. I, p. 653) says merely that "he sent to *Mercure de France* an article, 'Answer to a Questionnaire on the Fate of Religion.'" But as with all embarrassing matters, the *Chronicle* gives no hint of the nature of the answer.

[19] On this see Bertram Wolfe, *Marxism: One Hundred Years in the Life of a Doctrine* (New York, 1965), pp. 369–70, 375–77.

light from three workingmen, allegorical representatives of the apostles John and Peter and the Archangel Michael, from whom he learns that God dies when men disagree, and that when the people have fused into one mighty force and freed themselves from all discord and disharmony, they will resurrect God out of their own midst as once before He came out of their midst as a carpenter in Galilee. At the novel's close Matvei witnesses a miracle performed not by a saint but by a procession of the people, a procession of which he has become a part: their faith, their emotional exaltation, and their collective will take possession of a paralyzed girl, enabling her to arise and walk. Now at last Matvei feels indissolubly bound up with the folk and knows that he is joining them in an endless forward march toward an unseen yet certain goal, the apotheosis of the people itself through its toil and its wonderworking into a single, unitary, all-knowing, all-powerful god.

That night, alone in the woods yet alone no more, Matvei's new-found faith opens his lips that his mouth may declare the praise of the god-in-process-of-creating-himself:

I saw the earth, my mother, in the space between the stars. . . .
And I saw her master—the omnipotent, immortal people. . . .
and I prayed:
Thou art my God and the Creator of all gods, weaving them out of the beauty of Thine own spirit, in the labor and the turmoil of Thy quest. Let there be no other gods beside Thee, for Thou art the one and only God, the worker of miracles.
This I believe and do confess![20]

Lenin's rage when he read this knew no bounds. He believed, or professed to believe, that this was not Gorky's thought, and that the naive author was being misled by the

---

[20] M. Gorkii, *Ispoved* (*The Confession*) in *Sobranie Sochinenii* (Moscow, 1961), Vol. V, pp. 304–05.

more sophisticated Bolsheviks, Bogdanov, Bazarov, and above all by Lunacharsky, three men whom Lenin, at that moment, was expelling from the co-leadership of his group. Lunacharsky had indeed been following a similar train of thought in a two-volume work, *Religion and Socialism* (1906–07), where, with far less artistry than Gorky, he mixed the history of religion, sociological analysis, and poetic enthusiasm, all culminating in an apotheosis of Marxism as a "natural, earthly, anti-metaphysical, scientific and human religion" destined to put an end to all "supernatural, transcendent, unscientific, fetishistic, authoritarian, hierarchical faiths," and in their place put the faith of man in his socialized self and in the endless development of his powers. Socialism needed this touch of religious ardor, Lunacharsky maintained, for "religion is enthusiasm, and without enthusiasm you can accomplish nothing."

Gorky had been cherishing this thought for many years, but publicly, it was a critical review of Gorky's *Ispoved* by Lunacharsky that Lenin chose to attack, for "propagating a current which breaks with the foundations of Marxism . . . and wages war against proletarian, Marxian socialism."[21]

In tactful, persuasive letters, Gorky remonstrated with Lenin, urging him to come to Capri to talk the whole thing over after the fashion of friends and comrades with those

[21] From a resolution adopted by a conference of the Bolshevik Center held in Paris in June 1909 (with Bogdanov and his comrades arbitrarily excluded in advance). Lunacharsky's review had sought to protect Gorky from the latter's heretical choice of the words "the people," which according to Marxist dogma would have made him a Narodnik. He pictured Gorky as exalting not the people but a collective man who, born amid the smokestacks and the machines, would be the core of Gorky's god and would "perform the real work of transforming men into mankind." Thus he thought to salvage Gorky's "Marxism." When the State Publishing House published A. Lunacharsky, *Articles on Gorky* (1957), it omitted this review completely. Gorky, it should be added, did not derive his idea of god-building from Lunacharsky, for as early as 1902 he had written to Andreev: "We will create a God for ourselves who will be great, splendid, joyous, the protector of life, who loves everyone and everything." Yershov, *Letters of M. Gorky and L. Andreev . . .* , p. 40.

against whom he was pronouncing anathema. At this Lenin waxed yet angrier:

> . . . to preach a degenerate agnosticism . . . to teach the workers "religious atheism" and the "deification" of the highest human potentialities (Lunacharsky) . . . no! that is too much. . . .

With Gorky as an artist he strove to be more indulgent:

> . . . I think that an artist can draw much that is useful for himself out of every philosophy. . . . *Even if it be an idealistic philosophy,* you can come to conclusions which will bring to the workers' party enormous usefulness. That's true. But all the same . . . your present article . . . you must rework. . . . Any other conduct on your part, i.e. a refusal to rework the article, or a refusal to collaborate in *Proletarii,* will lead, in my opinion, to a sharpening of our conflict . . . and to the weakening of the . . . cause of the revolutionary Social Democracy in Russia.[22]

On March 16, he again rejected an invitation from Gorky to come to Capri, "to talk with people who permit themselves to preach the unity of scientific socialism with religion, I *cannot* and will not. . . . I have already *sent to press*. . . . a formal declaration of war. The time for diplomacy has passed." He added tart greetings to Maria Fedorovna Andreeva—"she, I hope, is not for God, hah?"[23]

Finally even the tolerant Gorky lost patience and wrote to the editorial board of the publishing house Znanie, of which he was the leading spirit:

> . . . Concerning the publication of Lenin's book [*Materialism and Empirio-Criticism*]: I'm against it because I know the author. A great wise-man, a wonderful person, but a fighting-cock, he would only mock at a chivalrous act such as that. Let Znanie publish this book, and he will say: the fools!—and those fools will be Bogdanov, I, Bazarov, Lunacharsky.[24]

[22] Letter of February 25, 1908, *V. I. Lenin i A. M. Gorkii*, pp. 29–31.
[23] *Loc. cit.*, p. 38.
[24] *Ibid.*, p. 43.

At the same moment, Lenin was writing to his sister, "As to Znanie, I have almost given up hope. . . . We will have to look elsewhere. . . ."[25]

In his letter to Znanie, Gorky made clear that he was breaking with Lenin on philosophical matters and joining forces with those Bolsheviks whom Lenin was expelling as heretics:

. . . The dispute flaring up between Lenin and Plekhanov on the one hand and Bogdanov, Bazarov and Co. on the other is extremely important and profound. The first two, though they differ with each other on tactics, both believe in and preach historical fatalism; the other side preaches philosophical activism. For me it is clear on which side the greater truth lies. . . .[26]

Almost immediately thereafter, Gorky's reverence for culture as a redeeming force brought on a new dispute to sharpen the old. From his own earnings, and funds gathered from wealthy friends, Gorky started a school to bring culture and enlightenment to Russian revolutionary workingmen and to bring to his home on Capri a bit of Russia. The school would pay the students' way to and from Russia, maintaining them in lovely Capri while they studied. A railway clerk named Vilonov, who had been arrested and escaped many times, had been beaten by the police, and contracted tuberculosis in prison, came to live with Gorky while convalescing. He returned clandestinely to pick worthy students for the school, thirteen of whom finally arrived after all sorts of adventures en route. Bogdanov lectured them on political economy, Pokrovsky on Russian history, Lunacharsky on the history of socialism and revolutions, and on the history of art, Gorky on Russian literature, Alexinsky on the labor movement—no mean faculty, for Lenin was to pronounce Bogdanov's book the best text on political economy, and Pokrovsky

[25] *Ibid.*, p. 42.
[26] *Ibid.*, p. 43.

the best Marxist historian. He had called Gorky the best
proletarian artist, while Alexinsky had been Lenin's spokesman in the Second Duma, and Lunacharsky would one day
be his Commissar of Education.

With his longing to "unite all constructive elements,"
Gorky dispatched an invitation to Trotsky, who accepted
and took the workingmen on a guided tour of the Museums
of Vienna, but failed to show up at the Capri school; to Karl
Kautsky and Rosa Luxemburg, who declared themselves too
busy; to such Menshevik leaders as Martov, Axelrod and
Plekhanov, who did not appear either.

Of course Gorky extended a warm invitation to Lenin.
Ever a pugnacious factionalist, Lenin decided without investigation that the school was a faction plot against him, hence
against the Party, to be disrupted at all costs. In vain did the
school council (both students and faculty) invite Lenin to
come himself to teach, and to bring three other members of
his faction with him as teachers; in vain did they offer to
accept the "ideological control of the Bolshevik Center in
Paris," i.e. of Lenin. Lenin would be content with nothing
less than the explusion from the faculty of those whom he
was expelling from his faction—Bogdanov, Bazarov, Alexinsky, Lunacharsky, Pokrovsky, and all "god-builders" (which
perforce included the school's very founder) —as well as all
those who had opposed him recently on tactical matters concerning the Duma deputies. The school must be disbanded
on Capri, and all its students, without its faculty, must come
to him in Paris for their education.

There are no Bolsheviks among your instructors, [he wrote to
the bewildered worker-students]. The Island of Capri has already
become known even in general Russian literature as the literary
center of the god-builders. . . . He who goes to study Social
Democratism in Paris goes to study real Social Democratism. He
who goes to study on Capri goes to study a *special* factional

"science". . . . The school was organized on Capri expressly to *cover up* its factional character, to conceal the school from the Party.[27]

Poor Gorky, who detested politics and factionalism and who had organized the school to solace his loneliness for Russia and to further the culture of Russian workingmen, was thus forced into the very center of party squabbles. Though Lenin avoided using his name as much as possible, every attack on the Island of Capri was a stab in the heart of a man who had tried to turn his home—always a Grand Hotel for homeless or needy Russians abroad—into a school for Russian workingmen.

The school ran nearly five months. During the fourth month, Lenin's continuous bombardment of factional attacks, aided by a workingman among the students who was secretly a police agent (the police had standing instructions to "split, and split, and again split," which, for different reasons, was Lenin's motto also), persuaded five students to come to Paris to study. All they got there was a series of lectures by Lenin on "The Present Moment and Our Tasks" and a lecture on "The Agrarian Policy of Stolypin," but Lenin's aim was accomplished. *Proletarii* wrote a gloating finis to Gorky's dream in an article entitled "A Shameful Failure."

Immediately Lenin set about wooing Gorky away from the others, apologizing for having "mistakenly" regarded his motives, and those of Vilonov, as "exclusively factional."

I had all along thought, [he wrote] that it would be stupid for me to try to discuss in a friendly way with you. . . . Today I had a heart-to-heart talk with Vilonov both on party matters and on you, and I saw that I had been terribly mistaken . . . and I want firmly to press your hand. Through your talent as an artist you

[27] *Lenin,* Vol. XV, pp. 435–41.

have brought the workers of Russia so much that is useful and will continue to be of such great use that it is not at all permissible for you to surrender to the gloom induced by an episode in the faction struggle of us exiles. . . . I warmly press your hand and Maria Fedorovna's, for now I have the hope of meeting you again and not as enemies.

Luck was with Lenin; at that moment Lunacharsky's wife, who was Bogdanov's sister, quarreled with Gorky's wife, so that the sunny little colony on Capri broke up in personal squabbles. Then at last Lenin found it possible to go to Capri.[28]

Lenin and Gorky seemed to patch things up. Yet there was pain in Gorky's heart, and smoldering wrath in Lenin's. In November 1913, the storm broke again. This time Gorky's sin was a coy jest in which he told some intellectual "God-seekers" that they would "find no God for the moment" because none had as yet been "created." On reading this Lenin thundered:

What is this you're doing? It is simply horrible, really!

You write "But the quest for God must be postponed *for a while* (only for a while?) There is nothing to seek where you have not put anything. Without sowing you can't reap. You have no god, you have not *yet* (*yet!*) created Him. Gods are not sought, *they are created*. . . ."

So it turns out that you are against "the quest for God" only "for a while"!! . . . Against god-seeking only in order to replace it with god-building!! Now isn't it horrible that such a thing *should come from you?*

God-seeking differs from god-building no more than a yellow devil from a blue one. To speak of god-seeking not in order to

---

[28] The account of the school and the faction struggle around it is to be found in *Lenin*, Vol. XV, pp. 431, 432, 436, 437, 438, 440, 463; *Chronicle*, Vol. II, pp. 99–101; *Lenin*, Vol. XXXIV, pp. 353–54; *Otchet pervoi vysshoi shkoly dlya rabochikh* (*Report on the First Higher School for Workers*), (Paris, 1910).

Courtesy A. M. Gorky Museum, Moscow.

The Wanderer. Photo, Nizhni Novgorod, 1891.

Courtesy A. M. Gorky Museum, Moscow.

Master of the Vagabond Tale. Photo, Nizhni Novgorod, 1892.

Courtesy A. M. Gorky Museum, Moscow.

Gorky with his wife, Ekaterina Pavlovna Peshkova, and their son Maxim.
Photo, 1899.

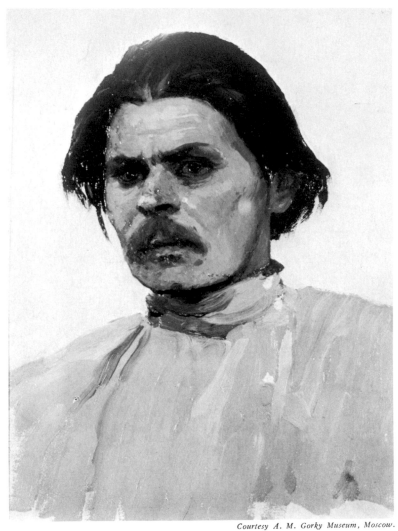

Courtesy A. M. Gorky Museum, Moscow.

Singer of the Stormy Petrel.
Portrait by M. V. Nesterov, Nizhni Novgorod, 1901.

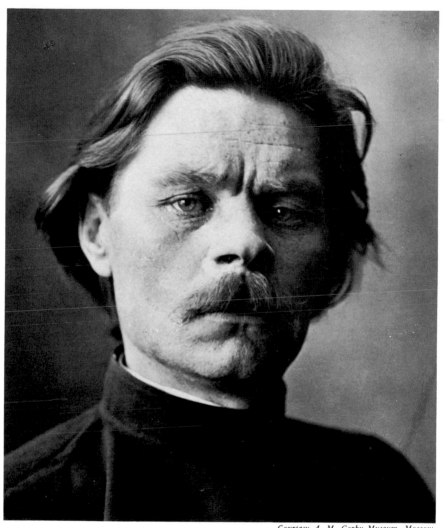

Courtesy A. M. Gorky Museum, Moscow.

The Author of the Lower Depths. Photo, 1901 or 1902.

From the Boris I. Nicolaevsky Collection of the Hoover Institution.

In the City of the Yellow Devil. Photo, New York, 1906.
Hitherto unpublished.

Courtesy A. M. Gorky Museum, Moscow.

Gorky in Capri. Portrait by O. Begas, 1911.

Courtesy A. M. Gorky Museum, Moscow.

The Curator of Russian Culture. Gorky at a Petrograd Railway
Station, bound for Moscow. Photo, 1920.

From the archives of the Hoover Institution.

At his desk in the editorial offices of "World Literature."
Photo, Petrograd, 1920.

From the archives of the Hoover Institution.

People's Commissar of Education A. V. Lunacharsky. Photo, 1920.

Courtesy A. M. Gorky Museum, Moscow.

Lenin and Gorky. Cutout from a photo of delegates and visitors
to the Second Congress of the Communist International.
Petrograd, 1920.

From the archives of the Hoover Institution.

V. I. Lenin in 1920. Photo with brushed-in background.

From the archives of the Hoover Institution.

Portrait of Lenin by N. A. Altman, May 1920.

Резолюция В. И. Ленина на заявлении С. П. Костычева, направленном А. М. Горькому о предоставлении материалов для его лаборатории.

Автограф.

Товарищи! Очень прошу Вас во всех тех случаях, когда т. Горький будет обращаться к Вам по подобным вопросам, оказывать ему в с я ч е с к о е содействие, если же будут препятствия, помехи или возражения того или иного рода, не отказать сообщить мне, в чем они состоят.

22 IV 1920 г. В. Ульянов (Ленин).

Holograph of Lenin's request that all assistance be given to Gorky in his works on behalf of the intelligentsia. The text reads:

Comrades! I urgently ask you on all occasions on which Comrade Gorky may address himself to you on such matters, to give him *every sort* of assistance; if there are obstacles, hindrances, or objections, of one sort or another, don't fail to report to me in what they consist.

V. ULYANOV (LENIN)
April 22, 1920.

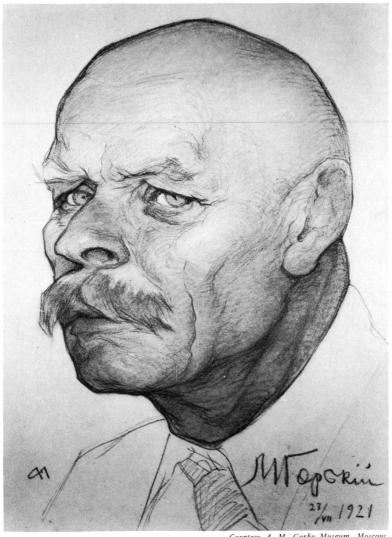

Courtesy A. M. Gorky Museum, Moscow.

Portrait of Maxim Gorky by N. A. Andreev, September 13, 1920, when Gorky was about to depart on his second exile.

Russkii revoliutsionnyi plakat (Moscow, 1925), p. 9.

"Help!" Soviet poster of 1921.

TELEGRAM

Washington, D. C.

July 23, 1921

Maxim Gorky, Petrograd:

I have read with great feeling your appeal to Americans for charitable assistance to the starving and sick people of Russia, more particularly the children. To the whole American people the absolute sine qua non of any assistance must be the immediate release of the Americans now held prisoner in Russia. Once this step has been taken the American Relief Administration, a purely voluntary association, and an entirely unofficial organization, of which I am chairman, together with other cooperative charitable American organizations supported wholly through the generosity of the American people have funds in hand by which assistance for the children and for the sick could be undertaken immediately. This organization has previously in the last year intimated its willingness to undertake this service as one of simple humanity disengaged absolutely from any political, social, or religious motives. However, for obvious administrative reasons it has been and is compelled to stipulate for certain undertakings. Subject to the acceptance of these undertakings we are prepared to enter upon this work. We are to-day caring for three and one half millions of children in ten different countries. This association would be willing to furnish necessary supplement of food, clothing, and medical supplies to a million children in Russia as rapidly as organization could be effected. The administrative conditions that we are obliged to make are identically the same as those that have been established in every one of the twenty-three countries where operations have been conducted one time or another in care of upwards of eight million children.

The conditions are that the Moscow Soviet authorities should give a direct statement to the Relief Administration representatives in Riga: (a) that there is need of our assistance; (b) that American representatives of the Relief Administration shall be given full liberty to come and go and move about Russia; (c) that these members shall be allowed to organize the necessary local committees and local assistance free from governmental interference; (d) that they shall be given free transportation of imported supplies with priority over other traffics; that the authorities shall assign necessary buildings and equipment and fuel free of charge; (e) that in addition to the imported food, clothing, and medicines the children and the sick must be given the same rations of such local supplies as are given to the rest of the population; (f) that the Relief Administration must have the assurance of non-interference of the government with the liberty of all of its members.

On its side the Relief Administration is prepared as usual to make a free and frank undertaking first that it will within its resources supply all children and invalids alike without regard to race, creed, or social status. Second, that its representatives and assistants in Russia will engage in no political activities.

I desire to repeat that these conditions are in no sense extraordinary but are identical with those laid down and readily accepted by the twenty-three other governments in whose territories we have operated.

HERBERT HOOVER.

From the archives of the Hoover Institution.

Cable from Herbert Hoover as Chairman of the American Relief Administration to Maxim Gorky, offering aid to the victims of the Russian famine. The text is reproduced from the press release issued on the same date.

From the Boris I. Nicolaevsky Collection of the Hoover Institution.

Holograph of unpublished letter of Maxim Gorky to Anatole France, appealing for pressure on the Soviet government to save the lives of the condemned Social Revolutionaries. The text reads:

Most esteemed Anatole France!

The trial of the Socialist revolutionaries is taking on the character of a public preparation of the murder of men who have sincerely served the cause of the emancipation of the Russian people. I urgently beg you: turn once more to the Soviet Government with the purpose of indicating the impermissibility of this crime. It may be that the weight of your influential voice may save the lives of these socialists. I am enclosing a copy of the letter which I myself am sending to one of the representatives of the Soviet Government.

With heartfelt greetings,

M. Gorkii

From the Boris I. Nicolaevsky Collection of the Hoover Institution.

Holograph of unpublished letter of Maxim Gorky to Alexei I. Rykov, Lenin's Deputy and Acting Chairman of the Council of People's Commissars. The letter reads:

Alexei Ivanovich!

If the trial of the Socialist Revolutionaries ends with a murder, it will be premeditated murder, an infamous murder!

I beg you to make this my opinion known to L. D. Trotsky and the others. I hope this won't surprise you, for you know that during the entire revolution I have indicated a thousand times to the Soviet Government how senseless and criminal it was to exterminate the intellectual forces in our illiterate and uncultured land.

Today I am convinced that if the Socialist Revolutionaries are executed this crime will result in the moral blockade of Russia by the socialists of all Europe.

M. Gorky

1/VII/22

Gorky always employed two distinct handwritings, the one a backward slanting print lettering for more formal and respectful letters as in the preceding letter to Anatole France, the other an impetuous forward-slanting cursive hand as in the present angry note to the more intimately known Rykov. The name of Lenin as the prime mover of the plan for the execution of the Socialist Revolutionaries is studiously omitted by the use of the formula "L. D. Trotsky and the others."

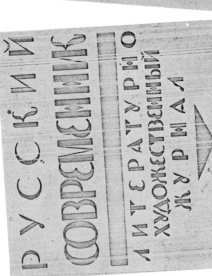

РУССКИЙ
СОВРЕМЕННИК

ЛИТЕРАТУРНО
ХУДОЖЕСТВЕННЫЙ
ЖУРНАЛ

№ 1

1924

М. ГОРЬКИЙ.

ВЛАДИМИР ЛЕНИН.

Владимир Ленин умер.

Даже некоторые из стана врагов его — честно признают: в лице Ленина мир потерял человека, «который среди всех, современных ему всяких людей, наиболее ярко воплощал в себе гениальность». Немецкая буржуазная газета «Prager Tageblatt», напечатав статью, полную почтительного удивления перед его колоссальной фигурой, закончила эту статью словами:

«Велик, недоступен и страшен кажется Ленин даже в смерти».

По тому статья ясно, что вызвало ее не физиологическое удовольствие цинично выраженное афоризмом:

«Труп врага всегда хорошо пахнет».

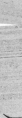

не та радость, которую ощущают люди, когда большой, беспокойный человек уходит от них,... нет, в этой статье громко звучит человеческая гордость человеком.

Лично для меня Ленин не только изумительно совершенное воплощение воли, устремленной к цели, которую до него никто из людей не решался практически поставить пред собою,— он для меня один из тех чудовищных, полусказочных и неожиданных в русской истории людей, каких был Петр Великий, Михайло Ломоносов, Лев Толстой и прочие этого рода. Я думаю, что такие люди возможны только в России, история и быт которой всегда напоминают мне Содом и Гоморру.

Для меня Ленин — герой легенды, человек, который вырвал из груди своей горящее сердце, чтоб осветить людям путь из позорного хаоса современности, из гнилого, кровавого болота разлагающейся «государственности».

Cover and first page of Gorky's article for *Russkii Sovremennik*, No. 1, 1924. Written from Sorrento immediately after Gorky learned of Lenin's death.

come out against all devils and gods, against all ideological copulation with a corpse (every bloody little god is copulation with a corpse . . .) —and to prefer a blue devil to a yellow one, is a hundred times as bad as not to say anything at all. . . .

Every religious idea, every idea of any little god, even every bit of coquettishness with a little god, is unutterable vileness. . . . A Catholic priest who violates a young maiden . . . is *much less* dangerous . . . than a priest without a cassock, without a crude religion, a priest full of ideas and democracy who preaches the construction and creation of little gods. For the first kind of priest is *easy* to expose, denounce, get rid of, while the second kind is *impossible* to get rid of so easily, and to expose him a thousand times more difficult. . . .

Really this is horrible. . . . Why do you do this? . . . This is hellishly harmful.[29]

Lenin had argued this all out with Gorky when he visited Capri in 1910, but Gorky had remained stubbornly silent, as he frequently did to avoid argument, a silence which Lenin had taken for assent. Hence he saw the new article as a "relapse," which helps to account for his fury. To appease him, Gorky apologized for having "let slip" the words, "postponed *for a while.*" But he did not yield in any other respect. Instead, without employing Lenin's angry and abusive tone, he offered a quiet defense of his views:

God is the complex of the ideas worked out by tribes, nations, mankind, which awaken social feelings and give them organized form with the aim of linking the individual personality to society, and of taming zoological individualism. . . . God-construc-

---

[29] *Lenin,* Vol. XXXV, pp. 89–91. Except in the words *bogostroitelstvo* (god-creation) and *bogoiskatelstvo* (god-seeking), which were technical terms of contemporary intellectual discussion, Lenin refused to use the word *bog,* (god), substituting throughout the letter a belittling diminutive, *bozhenka,* which defies translation by any English term that would convey his contempt. The nearest I could come to it in the most insulting sentence Lenin ever wrote to Gorky is to render it in English rather than in American fashion: "Every *bloody little god* is copulation with a corpse."

tion is the process of the further development and enlargement
of these social feelings in the individual and in society. . . .

At this, Lenin again hurled his anathemas: "reactionary
. . . idealistic . . . hocus-pocus . . . priestly . . . clerical . . .
lulling the class struggle to sleep . . . strengthening oppres-
sive class rule . . . simply horrible. . . ." But realizing how
deeply he had offended, he did not repeat the phrase *copulation with a corpse*.[30] This time Gorky did not answer.

On Christmas Eve 1917, with Lenin already in power and
incorporating militant atheism into the official religion of
the State as previously he had into that of his party, Gorky
wrote in *Novaya Zhizn:*

Today is the day of the birth of Christ, one of the two greatest
symbols created by the striving of man for justice and beauty.
Christ, the immortal idea of charity and humanity, and Prome-
theus, enemy of the gods, the first rebel against Fate—mankind
has not created anything greater than these two incarnations of
his aspirations. The day will come when in the spirits of men the
symbols of pride and charity, meekness, and unimaginable courage in the attaining of one's goals—both these symbols will fuse
into one great common feeling, and all mankind will recognize
its meaning, the beauty of its strivings, and the single corporeal
fusion of all men with one another.

In 1924, the year of Lenin's death, Gorky returned to this
theme with the words, "Only when the smithy is the church
of the blacksmith, the ship the church of the sailor, the
laboratory the church of the chemist, will it be possible for
men to live in such fashion as not to disturb the lives of
others by one's wickedness, one's whims, and one's habits."[31]

Finally in 1927, when Lenin's heirs asked Maxim Gorky to

[30] *Lenin,* Vol. XXXV, pp. 92–94.
[31] M. Gorkii, *Zametki iz dnevnika. Vospominaniya (Notes from My Diary.
Memories)*, (Berlin, 1924) , p. 57.

write an article for the tenth anniversary of the Bolshevik seizure of power, he showed he was of the same opinion still:

Years ago . . . I called man a god-builder, meaning that man, both within himself and in the external world, creates and incarnates the power to create miracles, justice, beauty, and all the other faculties with which Idealists endow a power alleged to exist outside of man. Man knows that outside himself there are no miracle-working forces. . . . He is certain that "only man exists, everything else being only his point of view and the work of his own hands." . . . It is this man who has undertaken the great task of educating the toiling masses "in his image and likeness."

There was no doctrinaire Lenin now to thunder against "little-god building" as "copulation with a corpse." Under the front-page heading of *Moi Privet ot MAXIMA GOR-KOGO* (My Greetings from MAXIM GORKY), the stubborn Gorky's heretical doctrine of god-building got at last into the sacrosanct pages of *Pravda* and *Izvestia*.[32]

[32] *Izvestia,* October 23, 1927; *Pravda,* November 6, 1927.

CHAPTER V

Of Truth and the Lie

Gorky grew up among evil, unhappy things. His art is a portrayal of other more attractive men than those his boyhood knew. His protagonists are closely and exactly observed, which gives them the breath of life, yet romanticized and made larger than life, which makes them into heroes. The gloom of the lower depths is brightened by bravado or pierced by some ray of hope, or some character is introduced who solaces the misery of the rest with a comforting illusion. In his key stories a streak of stubborn honesty about these consoling falsehoods causes Gorky to speak not in the euphemisms of *dreams* or *hopes,* but to spell out in its three uncompromising letters (four or five in Russian) the word *lie. Lgat'* and its various inflections appear in story after story; in one of his earliest tales the word is in the title itself. Always his attitude toward the comforting lie, and toward him who tells it, is ambivalent, yet on the whole rather more favorable than not. His cult of Man making himself into an omnipotent, omniscient, unitary god—or so Gorky permits himself to hope—is such a salutary lie: perhaps by believing in it and living by it, men may make it come true. This is Gorky's personal version of Utopia.

His first year's collection of short stories include the fable *Of the Finch that Lied and the Woodpecker, Lover of the Truth.* The weather having become permanently foul, the birds have lost their courage, their song has been reduced to the cacophonous cawing of crows. Then a plain little Finch calls attention to itself by singing sweet songs filled with courage, hope and faith, bidding the birds believe in the possibility of flying with him beyond the dark, stormy woods into a brighter clearing. But the Woodpecker, Lover-of-the-Truth, introduces the harsh reality principle that "no bird can fly higher than itself," and compels the Finch to confess that he has never seen the wondrous land of which he sings. The Finch breaks into tears, whereupon he is deserted and left alone with his thoughts.

Yes, I told lies, because I do not know what is there beyond the grove, but to believe and to hope is so good. . . . All I wanted was to awaken faith and hope. . . . Maybe the woodpecker is right, but what do we need of his truth when it weights our wings with stone, preventing us from flying into the sky?"[1]

The story is equivocal, yet it is clear that the author dislikes the Woodpecker with his nagging, petty truth, and sympathizes with the Finch.

The same problem reappears in a number of Gorky's writings, never ceasing to trouble him to the end of his days. It gets its richest development in his two long poetic works, the novel *Ispoved* (*The Confession*) , and the play *Na Dne* (*The Lower Depths*) . The connection of *Ispoved* with the problem is already clear, but we must return to *Na Dne* to examine this, the major of its two interwoven themes. The theme is one that has given us such great works of literature as *Don Quixote,* namely, the relationship between reality and illusion, but Gorky has given the theme a personal development of his own and constructed a variant peculiar to him. Far from being a protest or a realistic picture of life in the lower depths, *Na Dne* has as its central problem Truth and The Lie. It would be impossible, Gorky is saying, to live at the bottom of life without some consoling fiction concerning what life is, and what it may become.

[1] Cf. Pushkin's line in *The Hero:* "Tmy nizkikh istin mne dorozhe/Nas vozvyshayushchi obman. . . ." ("Dearer to me is the deception that elevates us than the darkness of base truths. . . .")

The main character is the wanderer, Luka. As soon as he appears, he begins to dispense his consoling gifts: equality ("you are all men"); solidarity or charity ("how can anybody cast off a human being? . . . It never does any harm to be gentle to a human creature"); interest in his fellows ("You're very curious, old man. You want to know everything—What for?" "To understand the affairs of human beings . . ."). Best of all, he offers a belief, however fragile, in a better life to come. At every moment of bitterness he offers comfort. When he perceives that the prematurely aged Anna is dying, he assures her that death is "easy on us and brings peace." The broken-down actor who commits suicide as the last curtain falls has been sustained for a while by Luka's assurance that one can give up alcohol (he actually does so until Luka has gone away) and that somewhere there is a sanitarium where they "treat you free of charge for they've decided that a drunkard is a human being." Under his encouragement, the actor remembers and declaims lines he has been striving to recall all through the play that touch on the central theme, lines that are poor poetry, but pure Gorky:

> If the world is unable to find . . .
> The road to justice and truth,
> Glory to the madman who weaves golden dreams
> Giving mankind surcease. . . .

On Vassya Peppel, the thief, Luka urges the belief that he can give up stealing. Peppel responds, "You lie mighty well old man. . . . Go on lying, there's little enough in this world that's pleasant." But he ends up saying, "I'll give up thieving. I swear I will. And I mean it. . . . I don't believe in conscience, yet one thing I do know—this is not the way to live. . . . I must live—in such a way that I can respect myself."

Natasha, sister-in-law and chief victim of the owner of the cellar-lodgings, is urged by Luka to escape with Peppel:

My advice to you, girlie—marry him. He's all right—he's a good fellow. Only you have to remind him as often as you can that he *is* a good fellow—so he doesn't forget it. He'll believe you. Just keep on telling him: *You're a good man.*

Just keep on telling him—that is Gorky's recipe for making men better. . . .

To the carpenter, Bubnov, Luka says, "It isn't always that truth is good for what ails a man—you can't always cure the soul with truth. . . ."

Luka's words of comfort reach their climax in an account of

a true and just land. There must be such a land. . . . The people there are of a special kind. . . . They respect one another, help one another, and everything they do is decent and fine. . . .

Gorky follows this with a wistful counterpoint:

LUKA. Yes, people keep looking—keep wishing for something better. God give them patience!
PEPPEL. What's your opinion, will they find it?
LUKA. Who, people? They'll find it. Look for something—want something with all your heart—and you'll find it.
NATASHA. If they would only find something—think up something good.
LUKA. They'll think it up. Only we have to help them, girlie—make it easier for them. . . .

Luka gave Marxist critics a lot of trouble. They tried to convince their readers that the cunning old pilgrim was a harmful figure, weakening the miserable by comforting dreams which tended to lead them away from that harsh reality out of which revolt should come. In their way the Marxist critics were right, for Gorky's formula for the im-

provement of society by each human being's improving himself and showing compassion to his neighbor, like his replac-
ing of class by Man, class hatred by love, reality by illusion,
was from their standpoint harmful indeed. Sensing this,
Gorky introduced an antagonist, Satín, the "official rea-
soner" or "counter-reasoner" of the play. Into his mouth
Gorky put the ritual formula:

> People weak in spirit—and those who live on the sweat of
> others—they need lies. The weak find support in them, the
> exploiters a screen. But a man who is his own master, who is
> independent and doesn't batten on others—he can get along
> without lies. Lies are the religion of slaves and bosses. Truth is
> the god of the free man.

But the heart has its reasons which reason knows not of.
Satín remains a colorless character until the last moment,
when after Luka has gone he rises to the old man's defense in
a succession of stirring speeches:

> "Shut up, you brutes, you numskulls! That's enough about the
> old man! . . . You understand nothing and lie. The old man is
> not a faker. What is truth? *Man*—that's the truth! He understood
> this—you don't. . . . Certainly he lied—but it was out of pity for
> you, the devil take you! There are lots of people who lie out of
> pity for others . . . lie beautifully, excitingly, with a kind of
> inspiration. . . .
> The old man had a head on his shoulders. He had the stirring
> effect on me of acid on a dirty old coin. Let's drink his health.
> . . . I asked him once, "Grandpa, what do people live for?"
> "They live for something better, my friend. . . ."
> Everybody lives for something better to come . . . working
> people—and peasants too, and even masters—they all live for
> something better to come. . . . That's why we have to be con-
> siderate of every man. Who knows what's in him, why he was
> born, what he can do? Maybe he was born for our greater
> benefit. . . .

Follows the famous apostrophe to Man ("it has a proud sound"), which we have already quoted in Chapter IV. It is clear that Luka has his author's affection, and that the antagonist Satín acquires it only when he rises to the old man's defense.[2]

The problem of truth and the lie was at the core of Gorky's spirit, and he never completely exorcised it. It was this ambivalence which led him at moments to abandon the age-old Russian quest for truth and justice (in Russian both are represented by a single word, *Pravda*), and to coin the unfortunate term, as if it contained the living "truth," of an "elevating" socialist future. His last and most important attempt to solve the problem came not in fiction but in a letter to E. D. Kuskova, written in 1929 when he was debating whether he should return to Stalin's Russia. Then he broke with this upright woman who had been his first guide into the world of learning and his lifelong friend, because she insisted on obtruding into his consciousness some painful truths. He broke with her to look to Stalin's Russia, of all places, for the comforting and salutary lie. His attitude toward Stalin's Russia is the tragic climax of his lifelong debate on truth and the lie. Then he would stake his reputation and his life on the "salutary lie," and lose the wager.

Here is the letter he wrote Kuskova when he broke with her and abandoned for several years the quest for truth for the uneasy solace of the "salutary lie":

You are accustomed to speak about facts that disgust you. For my part, I not only count it my right to keep silent about them, but I consider my ability to do so one of my chief virtues. . . . Immoral, you will say. So be it. The fact is that I hate sincerely and inflexibly that truth which is an abomination and a lie for

[2] For an interesting discussion of the relationship between Luka and Satín, see the sketch of Gorky by his friend, V. S. Khodasevich, in *Nekropol: Vospominaniya* (Brussels, 1939), pp. 250–53.

ninety-nine percent of the people. You probably know that during my stay in Russia,[3] I raised my voice in public, both in the press and at meetings of comrades, against *self-criticism*, against the habit of disturbing and blinding people with the poisonous and fatal dust of everyday truth. Without success, of course, but that does not dampen my ardor.

That other truth that excites in men confidence in their own will and reason is already sown in the minds of the masses, and with excellent results. What is important to me is the rapid all-round development of human personality, the birth of a new man of culture, of workmen in a sugar refinery who read Shelley in the original. . . .

Such men do not need the petty accursed truth in the midst of which they are struggling. They need the truth that they create for themselves. You may call me optimist, idealist, romantic. . . . That is your affair. Mine is to explain as well as I can why I am now *one-sided.*

How this strange truth which should spring from the salutary lie worked out for Gorky in Stalin's Russia falls outside the scope of the present story. . . .

[3] Gorky visited Russia briefly in 1928 for the official celebration of his sixtieth birthday.

CHAPTER VI

The Poison of Power

From 1906 to 1913 Gorky lived in exile from his native Russia and sought to make Italy his second home. He found its southern gaiety attractive, loved its Mediterranean light, took a child's delight in its fiestas, fireworks, music, animated talk, ready laughter, and thought his old homeland "gloomy and sad" in comparison; yet as a writer he felt as if his roots had been torn from their soil. "You must love Russia," he wrote to Andreev, "you must arouse her energy, her consciousness of beauty, her self-respect. She must be inoculated with a feeling of the joy of existence." As soon as Tsar Nicholas proclaimed a general amnesty in 1913 to celebrate the three-hundredth anniversary of the Romanov dynasty, Gorky hastened back with joy to his "sad and gloomy" motherland.

He came back to Russia, his friends reported, a "European," European in dress, in outlook, in praise of what he had seen in the West.

We Russians [he wrote to his friend Vladimir Posse] are always attracted by what is dark and evil. In our own obsession with evil we strengthen it around us, we hypnotize ourselves with it. In Europe we are always looking for what most resembles Russia, and when we find there filth, swindling, vulgarity, lies, we are content—*just like us!* It takes a Russian a long time to find out how Europe *differs* from us, in its stable and growing democracy, respect for individuals, capacity for discipline, organization, and productive work in the sphere of the spirit. . . . Our craving to pick out the dark and ugly strains in human character shamefully resembles the cunning philistine desire to drag everybody down to the lowest common denominator, to obliterate all bright colors and tones. . . .

One should write rather of what is good in the West, of that which may arouse envy, emulation, and other such forward-looking emotions and feelings in our citizens. In every letter from abroad our fellow citizens should see above all the advantages of Western life!

This was a new language for Gorky, and with it he developed a new critical attitude toward Lenin. To the former Leninist, Valentinov, he said shortly after his return to Russia:

Lenin is a remarkable man. And the Bolsheviks are vigorous people. But unfortunately there is among them too much squabbling over trifles, and squabbles are something I dislike. I dislike them greatly. Besides, they seek every opportunity to work underground, while I want to act not secretly but openly. All of us agree that we need a revolution and that it is necessary to enlighten the people politically. But that by itself is not very much. . . . We must teach the people literacy, culture, respect for work, knowledge of technology. It is necessary to give them a many-sided education. You see, we are hateful, backward Asia. Nothing good will come of us as long as we do not extirpate from ourselves the Asiatic spirit, as long as we do not become Europe.

Some two years later he wrote concerning culture a judgment which showed what a deep and wide abyss separated him from all that the "class-conscious" Lenin stood for:

The interests of all men have a common ground where they feel a common solidarity in spite of the inescapable contradictions of class friction. That ground is the development and accumulation of knowledge. Knowledge is that force which in the end must lead men to victory over the elemental energies of nature and the subordination of those energies to the common—cultural—interests of man.[1]

[1] N. Valentinov, "Vstrechi s M. Gorkim" (Meetings with M. Gorky) , *Novyi Zhurnal*, No. 78, 1965, pp. 138–39, pp. 124–25.

On his return to his homeland he found a new strong man to admire and work with, and to help him realize this dream of an all-human, classless culture, a self-made man like Gorky himself, with the same classless belief in man as man, the same deep, instinctive love of Russia, the same autodidact's reverence for culture in all its forms and all its works. The publishing giant I. D. Sytin was the owner of a great empire he had built up himself, an empire of newspapers, magazines, book-publishing concerns, paper mills, woodpulp forests, and withal, with unlimited funds and unlimited faith and good will to put at Gorky's disposal for nothing less than the general enlightenment of the Russian people.

To be sure, world war was soon to put an unbearable strain on this as on all the other resources of Russia. Still, with Sytin's help and his own earnings, Gorky remained throughout the war the publisher of a journal and the head of a publishing house. Though his "classless cultural deviation" angered Lenin, it was to Gorky's publishing house that the Bolshevik leader turned for the publication of his *Imperialism*.

To make legal publication possible, Lenin had written the work carefully, in "Aesopian language," applying his strictures to the German Empire and the British, but not to the Russian. But at this point not the Tsar's censors but Maxim Gorky as publisher demanded that he clean up the work by expunging the abusive language he had used against Karl Kautsky! Gorky respected Kautsky because the editor of *Die Neue Zeit* had refused to support the German government at war, remaining a pacifist and an internationalist. But "Kautsky is the most dangerous of all," Lenin had written of him at the war's outbreak, since Kautsky was competing with him in opposition to the war, yet did not favor "turning the imperialist war into a civil war," nor "the defeat of one's own government," nor the destruction of the Second International, but rather a struggle for an early return to peace and socialist unity. From 1914 on Lenin never let slip an opportunity to attack Kautsky, whom previously he had so admired and praised. Yet to assure publication, he swallowed his rage at Gorky and crossed out the abusive epithets.[2]

Gorky's continued friendliness toward Lenin during the war was the product of an elaborate misunderstanding. He was deeply shocked when he finally comprehended that Lenin's rejection of the war involved not a desire for an early peace, but a call for the defeat of Russia, and for the prolongation of the carnage by "turning the imperialist war into a civil war."

Gorky did not anticipate the sudden fall of the Tsar, nor did Lenin. But while Lenin rejoiced at the power vacuum which gave him his opportunity, Gorky felt fear. "With our inclination to anarchism," he wrote prophetically, *"we may devour freedom."*

The first days of euphoria and unity after the Tsar's downfall, gave him some hope. "The people have shown a high degree of consciousness," he wrote. "They have been wedded to freedom, and the marriage is indissoluble."

But he reckoned without partisan and factional strife, popular inconstancy and weariness. Above all, he reckoned without Lenin. When the latter returned to Russia in April 1917, and his *April Theses* were received with incredulous irony and contempt by all the parties in the Soviet and even by the leaders of Lenin's own party, Gorky continued to

[2] To Inessa Armand Lenin confided his indignation at this unexpected censorship: "My manuscript on imperialism has reached Peter[sburg], and today, you see, they write me that the publisher (and that means Gorky! Oh, the simple calf!) is dissatisfied with the sharpness of my expressions against . . . against whom do you think? . . . against Kautsky! Gorky wants to start up a correspondence to set me straight on that!!! It's both ridiculous and offensive." *Lenin,* Vol. XXXV, p. 209.

rejoice. "This is the best proof of how much political consciousness has risen in the people."[3]

In his journal, *Novaya Zhizn,* Gorky more than once de-
fended Lenin during 1917 against the charge of being a
German agent, but he refused even to see the man he had so
much admired, or to listen to a single address of the Bolshevik leader. Lenin's plans for an uprising against the new
revolutionary, democratic government, as outlined in his
April Theses and subsequent documents, were to Gorky incomprehensible and shameful. Since the Provisional Government had the grace to call itself *Provisional,* which meant it
regarded itself as merely pre-legitimate and would seek the
earliest opportunity to let the Russian people create their
own constitution and a new democratic legitimacy in a Constituent Assembly—and since in the meantime, all parties,
particularly all democratic and socialist parties, had complete freedom to organize and offer their programs—Lenin's
attempt to provoke civil war and establish a new dictatorship
and tyranny seemed to him apostasy and madness.

When Lenin seized power in October and put the democratic and liberal ministers of the Provisional Government
in the same Peter-Paul prison where the Tsar's police had
put leading revolutionists, the following scene occurred, as
described by the poetess Zinaida Hippius in her *Diary:*

Gorky was there. He gives a *terrible* impression. Gloomy, quite
dark, disheveled. He speaks as if growling from deep down. Poor
Mrs. Konovalov stands before him in great distress. (She is a
sweet little French girl, guilty before Gorky perhaps only because
her husband is a "bourgeois and a Kadet.") . . . He simply
refuses all intervention on behalf of the ministers. "I . . . person-

[3] Valentinov, *op. cit.,* pp. 128–29.

ally . . . find it impossible . . . to speak to those scoundrels, Lenin and Trotsky."[4]

Actually, Gorky did not visit Lenin for a year and a half, and then only because he was deeply moved when Lenin was wounded in the neck by a bullet from the pistol of Fanny Kaplan.

As early as October 18, 1917 (October 31 on the Gregorian Calendar in use in the West)[5] Gorky had warned Lenin against his contemplated seizure of power—an event still one week away.

Rumors are spreading [Gorky wrote] that on October 20th a "Bolshevik attack" will begin—in other words, the disgusting scenes of the 3rd and 5th of July may be repeated. . . . Once more big trucks jammed with armed men with rifles and revolvers in their trembling hands; from these guns they will shoot at shop windows, at people—at whatever they can hit! They will shoot because people thus armed want to kill their own fear. . . . All the dark instincts of the mob [will be] roused to fury by the deadly, destructive lies and filth of politics . . . which poison by their malice, hatred and vengefulness. People will kill each other because they are unable to destroy their own beastly stupidity.

---

[4] Z. Hippius, *Siniaya Kniga. Peterburgskii Dnevnik. 1914–1918* (Belgrade, 1929) , p. 233. Konavalov was the Minister of Commerce and Industry of the Provisional Government. Gorky denounced the incarceration of Konovalov and the other ministers in the columns of *Novaya Zhizn* one day after the reunion Zinaida Hippius here describes.

[5] The Soviet government continued to use the Old Style or Julian Calendar until February 14, 1918. The reader will have to add thirteen days to every date prior to February 1918 to get the corresponding Western date, for in the twentieth century the spread between the two calendars was of that magnitude. That is why the seizure of power of Lenin on November 7 by the Gregorian Calendar is regularly called the October Revolution (October 25, Old Style) . The quotations from Gorky which follow preserve the Old Style dating of his journal, *Novaya Zhizn*. When he published the little book of these attacks on Lenin in Berlin in 1920, he retained the dates on which they were published in *Novaya Zhizn*, and the same is true of their publication in German as *Ein Jahr Russische Revolution*, von Maxim Gorky, *Oktoberheft 1918 der Süddeutschen Monatshefte*, Leipzig and Munich, 1918.

Into the streets will creep a disorganized mob with no under-standing of what it wants. Behind and under the cover of this mob, adventurers, thieves, and professional killers will begin to compose the history of the Russian Revolution. . . . Who needs all this? and why? . . . The Central Committee of the Bolshevik Party is duty bound to repudiate these rumors.

On November 7 and 10, Old Style, that is on the thir-teenth and fifteenth days after Lenin's dictatorship began, Gorky signed his name to two prophetic open letters, one "To the Democracy," the other "To the Workingmen." In the first he expressed his indignation that Lenin had sent the democratic and liberal members of the Provisional Govern-ment to the Peter-Paul fortress. The Ministers, he wrote,

are now in the power of people who have not the slightest idea of the meaning of freedom of the person or the Rights of Man. Lenin and Trotsky and those who follow them are already poi-soned by the corrupting poison of power. This is proved by their shameful attitude toward freedom of the word [speech, press, assemblage], freedom of the person, and the whole sum of those rights for the triumph of which the democracy has been fighting. Blind fanatics and conscienceless adventurers are rushing at breakneck speed on the supposed road of "social revolution." . . . On this road Lenin and his comrades-in-arms consider it permissible to commit every sort of crime, such as the slaughters before Petersburg, the bombardment in Moscow [Gorky had in mind the bombarding of the Kremlin, which caused Lunacharsky to resign in tears from Lenin's Council of Commissars], the destruction of the freedom of the word, senseless arrests—all the vile things which in their day Plehve and Stolypin practiced against the Democracy.

In his appeal to the workers, Gorky wrote:

The working class cannot fail to understand that Lenin is only carrying out some sort of experiment on their hides, with their blood, striving to push to the last extremity the revolutionary mood of the proletariat and then see—what will come of it?

How well Gorky understood the man who only two weeks earlier had secretly written to his Committee, "The seizure of power is the point of the uprising; after the seizure, its political aim will clarify itself," and who, over half a decade later at the beginning of his final illness, could still write of his "experiment" in terms of Napoleon's military maxim, "on s'engage, et puis . . . on voit."[6]

Lenin knows Russia is not ripe for proletarian rule, Gorky continued, "yet perhaps he is hoping for a miracle." But the working class should understand that

miracles don't occur! What awaits them is famine, the complete breakdown of industry, the ruin of transportation, a long bloody anarchy, and, after it, a not less bloody and dark reaction. That is where their present leader is leading the proletariat, and they must know that Lenin is not an all-powerful magician, only a cold-blooded conjurer who will spare neither their honor nor their lives. . . .

Three days later, Gorky continued his prophetic warning:

Lenin is introducing into Russia a socialist regime after the fashion of Nechaev—full steam ahead through the swamp. Lenin and Trotsky and those who follow them to destruction are convinced with Nechaev that "with the right to dishonor you can best entice the Russian man to follow you," and so . . . they are forcing the working class to organize bloody butcheries, pogroms, arrests of people who are not guilty of anything. . . . By compelling the proletariat to agree to the destruction of freedom of the press . . . they are legalizing their own suppression; by threatening with starvation . . . all those who disagree with the Lenin-Trotsky despotism . . . they are justifying the despotism against which all the best forces in our land have so long struggled. . . .

[6] *Lenin*, Vol. XXVI, p. 204; Vol. XXX, p. 439.

Next Gorky gave a picture of Lenin as he knew him:

> He is of course a man of exceptional powers; for twenty-five years he has stood in the front ranks of the fighters for the victory of socialism. He is one of the greatest and most brilliant figures of the International Social Democracy. . . . He possesses all the characteristics of a *leader,* among them the traits indispensable for this leadership such as the absence of morality and a genuinely lordly lack of compassion for the life of the popular masses. Lenin is a leader and a Russian nobleman who does not lack the spiritual traits of that disappearing estate. That is why he believes that he has the right to perform a cruel experiment on the Russian people. . . . Exhausted and ruined by the war, the people have already paid for this experiment in thousands of lives and will have to pay with tens of thousands more. . . . This inevitable tragedy does not trouble Lenin, a slave of dogma, nor his zealous servitors. . . . Life in its complexity is unknown to him. He does not know the popular masses, for he has never lived among them. Out of books, he has learned . . . by what means to whip up their instincts most easily to a fury.
>
> For Lenin & Co. the working class is what ore is to the metallurgist. Let's see whether it is possible to pour off from this molten ore under the given circumstances a socialist state. Apparently not—but why not try? What does Lenin risk if the experiment does not succeed?

A month later Gorky answered an attack by *Pravda* in these words:

> To me it is a matter of indifference what they may call me for my opinion of this "government" of experimenters and visionaries, but the fate of the working class and of Russia, these are not matters of indifference to me. As long as I am able, I shall tell the Russian proletariat over and over again: "They are using you as material for an inhuman experiment; in the eyes of your leaders you are no longer regarded as human. . . ."

The bitterest blow to Gorky, as to all socialists and democrats who had so long struggled for freedom, was Lenin's dispersal of the Constituent Assembly by force of arms. The assembly was chosen by the first free election in the history of Russia, the first and up to now—a half century later—still the only free election. For, having used force to destroy the possibility of a free people's writing its own constitution and creating its own democratic legitimacy, Lenin and his successors would never thereafter be able to submit their actions to a free election or to the criticism of a free press.

For almost a hundred years [Gorky wrote] the best people of Russia have lived with the idea and hope of a Constituent Assembly—a political instrument which would give the whole Russian democracy the chance freely to express its will. . . . In the struggle for this idea, in dungeons, in exile, in penal labor, on scaffolds, under the bullets of soldiers, died thousands of intellectuals and tens of thousands of workingmen and peasants. . . . And now, here are "People's Commissars" ordering rifle fire against the Democracy which marches in a demonstration to honor this idea. . . .

Pravda lies [the words are more chilling in Russian for Pravda means The Truth, and Gorky is saying The Truth lies] when it writes that the demonstration of January 5th was organized by the bourgeoisie, bankers, etc. . . . Pravda lies—it knows very well that for the bourgeoisie there is no reason to rejoice at the opening of the Constituent Assembly, that they can do nothing in the midst of 246 socialists [most of them members of the Socialist Revolutionary Party] and 140 Bolsheviks. Pravda knows that the workingmen of the Obukhovsky Factory, the Munitions Factory, and other workshops took part in the demonstration, that under the red banners of Russian Social Democracy from the Tauride Palace marched the workers of the Vasillyostrov District, the Vyborg District, and other proletarian districts. These same workingmen are the ones who were shot down. . . . No matter how much The Truth lies, it will not be able to get rid of this shameful fact.

At the end of six weeks in power, Gorky told Lenin, you have produced a rash "of meaningless decrees written with a fork on water[7] . . . and up to ten thousand lynchings."

When a Bolshevik wrote him publicly, "You ought to rejoice, the proletariat has been victorious," Gorky answered on December 19:

There's nothing for me to rejoice at; the proletariat has not won a victory in anything or over anybody. . . . The victorious [can] as a rule be magnanimous. . . . But the prisons are full of people, one does not know why, and thousands—yes, thousands!—of workingmen and soldiers are starving. . . . There is no sign that a revolution has inspired in the masses a social feeling toward others. "The new authorities" are as crude and brutal as the old, only even less well educated. . . . There is no poison more terrible than power over one's fellowmen: we must remember this lest power now poison us, transforming us into cannibals even more vile than those against whom we have been fighting all our lives.

Gorky's column, frequently headed simply "Untimely Thoughts," became gloomier and gloomier as he watched the spread of famine and disease, the death of countless intellectuals from cold, neglect, and starvation. The intellectuals were being given still more meager rations than the miserable few ounces of bread distributed to soldiers and industrial workers. Moreover, unlike the latter two classes, they had no way of "requisitioning" bread or trading "the people's" tools on the Black Market. By permitting these intellectuals to die, Gorky wrote, we are destroying "the spiritual capital of the Russian people." "We are breeding,"

[7] Lenin himself was to admit to the Eighth Congress of his party on March 23, 1919, that he knew the decrees were unrealizable but considered them useful as "propaganda." *Lenin*, Vol. XXIX, pp. 185–86.

too, "a new crop of brutal and corrupt bureaucrats and a terrible new generation of youth who are learning to laugh at daily bloody scenes of beatings, shootings, cripplings, lynchings." Gorky's prose was more powerful than ever but not fiction now.

In the spring things grew worse. Late in May of 1918 he described: "a woman doctor, who has devoted her whole life as a *zemstvo* physician to the service of mankind. Dying of hunger, helpless, dirty, absolutely alone, dying in a frightful room . . . *Starving* [she said] *is much more terrible than I thought. . . .*" Readers took some part of their poor rations to him to help this woman, but by then "her body was all but destroyed by hunger and lice."[8]

Professor Gezenko, famous physicist, aged seventy-five, was dying of starvation.

. . . though the great French Revolution chopped off the head of the chemist Lavoisier, it did not starve its scientists to death. . . . To the cynic who might say, "Why bother? After all, the Professor is 75," I answer—In the same Obukhov hospital, starving, are 134 men, more than half of them manual workers between twenty and thirty, needing 3,000 calories per day, and getting from 5 to 600, much of it in indigestible form. . . . Every day people are picked up on the streets where they have dropped from hunger. . . . Intellectuals are losing weight faster than the others. . . . Their capacity for mental work will soon be exhausted, but our country needs such people more than ever. . . . Petrograd . . . the center of our intellectual life . . . is a dying city.

On June 8 he wrote "The Sick City," a terrible picture of famine in Petrograd, a vivid account of how a girl, a boy, a cat, a horse, and a former officer acted while dying of hunger.

On June 9 he told of going to the zoo (he might have said dragging himself, for he too was hungry and was bleeding

[8] *Novaya Zhizn*, May 23 and June 1, 1918.

from the lungs). He described the puzzled, submissive, pleading animals, the dying lions, tigers, elephants, snakes. In late June, touring the villages, he found "the ghost of famine silently hovering over the . . . once grain-rich land." He described soldiers seizing grain to sell. They were fired on by a second military detachment, which itself sold the grain to the cooperative owned by the very peasants from whom it had been seized in the first place. In Nizhni, Orel, Penza, Samara, no one was sowing grain because all the seed had been "requisitioned."

How to silence this fearless, incorruptible man? Lenin tried demonstrations and strikes at *Novaya Zhizn*'s printing plant, but the journal continued to come out with Gorky's "Untimely Thoughts," and, as the sole mouthpiece of voiceless millions, its circulation continued to grow. Lenin cut off the paper supply; Gorky imported newsprint from Finland. *Pravda* attacked Gorky's funds as coming "from the bourgeoisie"; we have seen how effectively Gorky answered.

The Bolshevik fraction in the Putilov plant sent him a warning that they would shut down his paper "by direct action" if he did not cease his polemics. Gorky published their threat on December 22, and answered, "We will continue our polemics with the government which is leading the working class to its ruin. We hold this to be our duty—the duty of every honest citizen, of every independent socialist."

I have no doubt that Lenin suffered as he read these dreadful reports from Gorky's pen, for he knew they were true and came from a man whose honesty he could not question. Gorky suffered even more with every word he wrote. Many a time in the past he had unashamedly shed tears as he read aloud some moving scene from one of his own tales; now his tears blotted the manuscript pages of his articles. Between these two friends, each doing his duty as he saw it, the conflict had become a conflict of wills. In such a conflict Lenin was the stronger. Sustained by dogma, he was willing to have Russia suffer anything to bring about the imminent European revolution he was so sure would come.[9]

On July 16, 1918, having long ago silenced all other democratic and socialist journals, Lenin gave the order that the voice of Maxim Gorky, too, be stilled.[10] Unlike the situation under the last Tsar, there was thenceforth to be no journal not owned by the same people who were the censors, the one-party state. For many months Gorky could get no word into the press, not even to answer its attacks upon him. For the first time in his life as a writer, there was no journal in Russia in which he might continue to fulfill his "obligations as a citizen and an independent socialist." This great writer —never as great as is now claimed, but surely a writer of great talent and civic valor—was in a fair way to becoming an unwriter in his native land.

Yet Gorky loved the man he was excoriating, and who was stifling his voice the better to carry on unchecked his experiment on Russia. A would-be assassin's bullet that gravely wounded Lenin in the neck on August 30, 1918, stirred the sentimental Gorky to visit the dictator. Looking into his visitor's suffering eyes, Lenin knew he had won an advantage. Wounded though he was and scarcely able to talk, he could not forbear following it up.

Our meeting [Gorky recollected in 1924][11] was quite friendly, but all the same the penetrating, all-seeing eyes of Ilyich gazed at

[9] To the Eighth Congress in March 1919, Lenin said that "the Soviet power puts the world dictatorship of the proletariat and the world revolution above any and every kind of national sacrifice, no matter how painful it might be." *Lenin*, Vol. XXIX, p. 128. His writings of 1918 and 1919 are full of the expectation that at any moment this grim gamble in which he was playing *Vabanque* with Russia would be won.

[10] On this see *V. I. Lenin o literature i isskustve* (Moscow, 1957), p. 599; *V. I. Lenin i A. M. Gorkii* p. 322.

[11] Gorky, "V. I. Lenin." Gorky wrote his celebrated memories of Lenin immediately after the latter's death, shedding copious tears on the pages of

me, "the erring one," with visible regret. A look that was very familiar to me—he had been looking at me that way for thirty years. The same look, I am convinced, will follow me to my grave. Let not the reader regard it as boasting: I don't want to suggest that it is precisely the "erring ones" who discover new paths and Americas; still it is always easier for me to agree with people out of respect for them, or even out of politeness, than out of a compulsion clear to them and unclear to me.

After a few minutes, Lenin said heatedly:

"Who is not with us is against us. People independent of history is a fantasy. . . . No one needs them. . . . You say that I simplify life too much. That this simplification threatens culture itself, eh? . . . And in your opinion, millions of peasants with rifles in their hands—that's not a threat to culture? You think the miserable little Constituent Assembly [Lenin expresses his contempt by coining the untranslatable neologism *Uchredilka*] could have handled their anarchism?". . .

Lenin began using skillfully Gorky's own opinions, showing how carefully he had studied the attacks on his dictatorship in *Novaya Zhizn*. He proposed a sort of armistice. Gorky would have to accept his regime sufficiently to work with it (inside "history") . He in turn would permit Gorky to devote himself to the patriotic task closest to his heart, namely the saving of Russia's intelligentsia and Russia's culture, under the harsh conditions of dictatorship and famine.

"A union of the workingmen and the intelligentsia," eh? That's not bad, not bad at all. Tell the intelligentsia—let them come over to us. . . . Do you suppose I dispute [your] contention

his manuscript ("Even more than I grieved over Tolstoy's death," he wrote to Andreeva) , and published it in *Russkii Sovremennik*, No. 1 (March 1924) , 229–44. Since the work has been so often changed and doctored before getting worldwide distribution under Stalin, I have drawn my quotations as far as possible from this original version, which was completed a month after Lenin's death and entitled simply Vladimir Lenin , with a black border around the name.

that we need the intelligentsia? But—you see how hostile they are. . . . And it will be their own fault if we deal too harshly with them [literally: "if we break too many pots"].

Gorky accepted the truce. He did not give up his reservations concerning Lenin's "ruthless experiment," and his dispersal of the Constituent Assembly by force of arms, and his seizure of power. But he ceased his criticism so long as he remained inside Russia, accepting Lenin's power insofar as he could use it and, by appealing to it, might mitigate the terror and famine and save what he could of Russia's intellectuals and Russia's culture.

CHAPTER VII

Curator of Russian Culture
I: The Great Entrepreneur

When Gorky died, Leon Trotsky wrote an obituary somewhat patronizing in tone but showing considerable insight into the artist's spirit:

Deeper than anything else in this unusual autodidact was rooted a worshipful attitude toward culture; his first contact with her, so to speak, burned a brand on his spirit for the rest of his life. . . . In his relations with culture there always remained more than a little fetishism and idolatry. To war Gorky took the approach above all of fear for the cultural values of humanity. . . . The Revolution of 1917 Gorky met with trepidation, almost like the director of a museum of culture: "unbridled" soldiers and "idling" workers inspired in him direct terror. The stormy and chaotic uprising of the July Days evoked in him only disgust. . . . The October Revolution he met as a direct enemy. . . . It was very hard for Gorky to reconcile himself with the fact of a victorious upheaval: in the land ruin prevailed, the intelligentsia was starving and suffering persecution, culture was or seemed to be in danger. In those first years he acted primarily as an intercessor on their behalf before the revolution. Lenin, who valued and loved Gorky greatly, feared that he would become a victim of his connections and his weaknesses, and finally managed to arrange his voluntary exit to a foreign land.[1]

However amusing a professional revolutionist like Trotsky might find concern with cultural values at a moment when a world was ending, it is one of Gorky's greatest glories

[1] *Byuleten Oppozitsii,* July–August 1936.

that amidst war and civil war, he did continue to concern himself with Russian culture, and with the lives of those intellectuals who were its embodiments, creators, and transmitters. On the morning Lenin seized power, Gorky's signed column in *Novaya Zhizn* bore the title CULTURE IS IN DANGER! Many had the same thought, yet none but he had the reverence, the tireless energy, the dogged determination, and, as it turned out, the connections, which might enable him to do something about it.

The task Gorky took upon himself was anything but easy. Lenin, through whom he had to work, was the very eye and center of a storm of class war and civil war. For the new ruler of Russia, "bourgeois intellectuals" included all who opposed him and his dictatorship ("Who is not with us is against us"), all who were neutral, all who questioned the principle of dictatorship or favored democracy, all who supported some brand of socialism other than his own. Even totally nonpolitical scholars were superfluous and suspect. Rations were brutally short for the newly proclaimed elite—workingmen, soldiers, and Communist officials. If these were hungry, what then was the plight of the intellectuals whose ration category was far lower than theirs?

I saw men and women [wrote Angelica Balabanoff of Russia during this period] who had lived all their lives for ideas, who had voluntarily renounced material advantages, liberty, happiness, and family affection for the realization of their ideals— completely absorbed by the problem of hunger and cold.[2]

If that was the condition of veteran Bolsheviks, one can imagine the lot of the non-party intellectual. Those who engage in intellectual labor are not known as a rule for their physical strength. One of the decrees the new ruler himself drafted, in the first month after his seizure of power, pro-

[2] Balabanoff, *My Life as a Rebel* (New York, 1938), p. 204.

vided for "universal labor service," and obliged citizens of both sexes "to perform the work assigned to them by local Soviets . . . or other organs of the Soviet power." To those who "had been naught and now were all," no work was acceptable as "social labor" for intellectuals except manual work. And since intellectuals were without industrial skills, this meant they were assigned only the most menial sort of manual work. As late as August 1920, Alexander Kaun reports, "one could still read an announcement on the walls of the Academy of Sciences to the effect that every employee, from scientist to doorman, was to take turns watching for six hours at a stretch the firewood stacked on the pavement in front of the Academy."[3]

The conditions under which dedicated intellectuals, writers, and artists were continuing their work at the moment Lenin and Gorky made their pact are impossible to convey to the reader. The great physiologist and psychologist, Pavlov, later to be exhibited as one of the glories of Russian culture, performed his experiments and gave his lectures to cold and hungry auditors while working without heat or electric light, shivering in a fur coat, fur cap and gloves. He planted potatoes for his own nourishment and fed his experimental animals the bits of salt fish or other proteins that fell to his lot, complaining only of the waste of precious hours and strength on the performing of the janitorial duties that were assigned to him as "socially useful labor."

When H. G. Wells visited Russia in 1920 he found the composer Glazunov pale, emaciated, ragged: yet all he asked was that Wells send him paper on which he might note down the music he composed in his head. Poets, philosophers, scientists, historians, mathematicians wrote their reflections, research and compositions on cigarette paper, on toilet pa-

[3] For the decree see *Lenin*, Vol. XXVI, p. 353; for the placard see Alexander Kaun, *Maxim Gorky and His Russia* (New York, 1931), pp. 484–85.

per—until the latter disappeared altogether—on scraps of wrapping paper, in microscopic letters. They burned their furniture and the wood of their floors for warmth, sold precious possessions for a pittance to get food or firewood or materials for work, yet held on stubbornly to those few things that their work required for its continuance.

Gorky's sacrifice was greater than any, for he gave up the writing which was his very life, to dedicate himself to saving the lives of others. Often he, too, was hungry, sick, and sick at heart, as he struggled with his huge self-imposed task. Here is a typical day in the life of this friend and favorite of Lenin's, as he narrated it to Kaun:

> Morning. Scurvy, your teeth are loose, you hate to get up. You come down to the dining room and find two or three dozen complainers, cold and hungry people. You call at the Scholars' Home, or the Commission of Experts on Art Treasures. . . . You sit on the curb and remain there for half an hour, forty minutes . . . only to stay away from the damnable mess.[4]

Gorky's first concern was with Lenin himself, dominant partner in the pact and all-powerful ally and intercessor, yet a chief source of danger as well. With reckless fury and demagogy Lenin and his lieutenants were inciting the masses against the *burzhui*. For the masses of the great cities—and for the village poor to whom Lenin was soon to appeal—all those in black coats, no matter how threadbare, were *burzhui*. Even the wearing of eyeglasses was enough to mark one as a *burzhui*.[5] In print and in speeches Lenin called for "street justice," for the setting up of impromptu "revolution-

---

[4] Kaun, *op. cit.*, p. 497. With the Scholars' Home and the Commission of Experts on Art Treasures we are running ahead of our story, for they were two of the devices in the great complex of life-and-culture-saving inventions that Gorky contrived in the course of his efforts to conserve Russia's culture.

[5] On eyeglasses as the mark of a *burzhui*, see Sergei G. Pushkarev, "1917—A Memoir," *Russian Review*, January 1967, p. 66.

ary tribunals," for raiding parties, for firing squads to "shoot on the spot those hiding anything."

To get a notion of the atmosphere Lenin was creating, one need only read his draft of what, with unconscious irony, he entitled, "How to Organize Competition":

> Each commune, each village, each city, should show initiative and inventiveness in devising ways of *cleansing* the Russian land of noxious insects, scoundrel fleas, bedbug rich, and so forth. In one place they will put into prison a dozen rich men, a dozen scoundrels, a half-dozen workingmen who shirk on the job. . . . In another they will set them to cleaning outdoor toilets. In a third, give them yellow tickets [such as prostitutes were given] after a term in prison . . . so that the entire people may act as overseers over them as harmful people. In a fourth they will shoot on the spot one out of every ten guilty of sloth. . . . The more varied these devices, the better . . . for only practice will work out the best measures. . . .

Fortunately, this terrifying document (pp. 367–76 in his *Collected Works*, Vol. XXVI) was written while Lenin was on a five-day vacation in Finland, and he had time for second thoughts, which led him to withhold it from publication. But his works abound in other incitements to lynch law, that were published as he struck them off in the heat of his fury.[6]

Besides incitements to spontaneous and impulsive violence, Lenin drafted decrees for search and seizure parties to be made up of workers, poor peasants, and soldiers. On January 27, 1918, he demanded that the entire working class join these detachments in the hunt for "speculators" or "bagmen" (peasants who carried in a bag to the town some of their produce to trade it for urban things they needed).

---

[6] For such incitements see *Lenin*, Vol. IV, pp. 368–69; Vol. IX, pp. 389–93; Vol. XXIII, pp. 279–80; Vol. XXVI, pp. 266, 375, 557–59. See also the analysis of this side of Lenin's temper in Wolfe, "Leninism," in *Marxism in the Modern World*, Milorad Drachkovitch, ed. (Stanford, 1965), pp. 69–76.

Every factory and every regiment must pitch in to set up "several thousand raiding parties of ten to fifteen people each."

Regiments and factories which do not accurately set up the required number of detachments will be deprived of bread cards and subject to revolutionary measures of persuasion and punishment. . . . Speculators caught with the goods . . . will be shot on the spot by the detachments. As long as we do not apply terror—shooting on the spot—we won't get anywhere.[7]

In late December 1917 or early in 1918, Lenin laid the foundation for more organized and systematized terror by putting Dzerzhinsky at the head of a new Extraordinary Commission for the Combatting of Counter-Revolution and Sabotage. The spirit in which this new Commission, known by its initials as the *Cheka,* started its work is suggested by the first number of its house organ, the journal *Krasnyi Terror (Red Terror),* in which its Chairman for the Ukraine, Martyn Ivanovich Latsis, wrote:

We are not waging war against individual persons. We are exterminating the bourgeoisie as a class. During the investigation, do not look for material and proofs that the accused acted in *deed* or *word* against the Soviet power. The first questions that you ought to put are: To what class does he belong? What is his origin? What is his education or profession? And it is these questions that ought to determine the fate of the accused. In this lies the significance and "essence of the Red Terror."[8]

All at the same time, the new "curator" had to concern himself with preserving cultural and artistic monuments from the ignorance and barbarism of the aroused mobs, with protecting the lives of intellectuals from hunger and cold,

[7] *Lenin,* Vol. XXVI, pp. 457–59.
[8] *Krasnyi Terror,* No. 1, November 1, 1918. A run of this short-lived journal is in the collection of the Hoover Institution. The Latsis article was reprinted in *Pravda,* December 25, 1918.

the Cheka, and impromptu firing squads, and with the working out of some system of institutions whereby they might
continue to follow their interests and live by them, or get
some employment at least related to their skills. Again and
again he had to argue with Lenin and plead for his signature
on some order saving the life of one of the victims of the fury
that breakdown and civil war and Lenin's own incitements
and sweeping orders had unleashed.

Gorky had seen outbursts of capricious cruelty and brutality before, coming from the *Lumpenproletariat* who lent
themselves most readily to the formation of urban mobs and
raiding parties, or from the peasants, particularly the
ne'er-do-well, rootless "peasant poor" to whom Lenin was
even then appealing. He remembered his flight into the
flame-lit darkness with his Narodnik benefactor, Romas,
from malevolent arson and a pursuing mob at Krasnovidovo
in 1888. He remembered how he had been beaten unconscious by a peasant mob at Kandubovka in the Gubernia of
Kherson in 1891. He remembered the pogroms of 1903 and
1906 when, surreptitiously incited by a few police officials,
vodka-sodden mobs had killed "students and Jews." But
never before had violence been urged thus openly, persist-
ently, pedantically, by the supreme ruler of the land, nor
been advocated in the name of socialism and justice. And
these new mobs or "detachments" were still wearing their
ragged uniforms, still bearing rifles, and were accustomed by
war to death's harvest. Lenin's articles and decrees seemed to
them a license to break into any home, seize any object of
value, and sully whatever looked useless or simply alien to
them.

With particular anguish Gorky watched Lenin's incite-
ment of the village poor.

The village has ceased to be united [Lenin told the First
All-Russian Congress of Deputies of these bodies that he was

calling into being]. . . . The formation in the village of Committees of the Poor has been the turning point to bring into the village the conscious socialist struggle. . . . From this union of the village poor with the city proletariat will come the decisive struggle against capital in all its forms. . . .

To the first of the regional congresses of such deputies Lenin declared; "These Committees must cover the whole of Russia. . . . We shall merge the Committees of the Poor with the local Soviets, we shall turn the Committees of Poor Peasants into Soviets."[9]

In short, these were to be the lords of the countryside, as the armed workingmen were to be lords of the city. Clearly the new self-appointed, and Lenin-approved "Curator of Culture" would have his hands full.

Gorky watched ruefully as the elect of the Village Poor of the Northern Province assembled in Petrograd. After attending their sessions from the third to the ninth of November, and being chosen along with Lenin an honorary member of their presidium, he wrote:

From the northern provinces came several thousands of peasants. Of these, hundreds were lodged in the Winter Palace of the Romanovs. When the Congress was over and these people gone, it turned out that they had polluted not only all the bathtubs of the palace, but an enormous number of precious vases as well—Sèvres, Saxon, and Oriental—which they had used as nightpots. This was not done out of necessity—all the toilets were in good order and the waterpipes functioning properly. No, this hooliganism was an expression of the desire to spoil, to deface, to sully beautiful things. During two revolutions and wars, hundreds of times I have observed this dark, vengeful striving of the people to

<hr>

[9] Lenin's address to the representatives of the Village Poor assembled in Petrograd has been preserved only in a newspaper account. His addresses to the Moscow Conference and the All-Russian Conference, in November and December 1918, respectively, are given in full in *Lenin*, Vol. XXVIII, pp. 152–58, 314–325.

break, corrupt, mock, shame whatever is beautiful. . . . The evil urge to spoil things of exceptional beauty comes from the same source as the shameful striving to vilify any exceptional human being.[10]

He brought to the Commissar of Education, Lunacharsky, an *Appeal to the Citizens of Russia*. Actually he had written it earlier and it had been posted and circulated before by the Soviet Executive Committee which Lenin overthrew, but now Lunacharsky posted it again. It read:

Citizens, the old masters are gone, leaving behind them an enormous heritage. Now it belongs to the entire people. Citizens, protect this inheritance. Protect the palaces, they will become palaces of your national art. Protect the pictures, statues, buildings, those incarnations of your spiritual strength and that of your ancestors. Art is the beauty which men of talent have known how to create even under the yoke of despotism. Do not touch a single stone. Protect the monuments, the buildings, the ancient objects, the documents. All these are your history, your pride. Remember, this is the soil from which your new national art will grow.

To make sure that the citizens heeded, and that there would be some place to store the treasures (and some steady employment for a few "superfluous" intellectuals whose only skill was a knowledge of art), Gorky persuaded the Commissar of Education to make him the head of a Commission for the Protection of Museums, Art Objects, and Historical Monuments.

Working on this task of conserving art objects, he soon discovered that he had to contend not only with destructive impulses of the masses, but with Lenin himself, and with Lenin's commissars and confidential agents, for they were sending raiding parties to homes and churches to seize ikons,

---

[10] *V. I. Lenin i A. M. Gorkii*, p. 240.

vestments, sacramental vessels, statuary, jewels, ceramics, paintings, not to conserve them but to sell them abroad for hard cash. Quietly, undemonstratively, Gorky himself began to appear on the Black Market with royalties sent him from abroad, to buy for a pittance precious things to adorn his own quarters. His home became an art museum, causing some to charge that he had made a deal with Lenin in order amidst universal misery to live in splendor. He wrote nothing to defend himself and said nothing to Lenin. But when the time of general pillage had passed and things of beauty were no longer in imminent danger, except for a few small objects he had given to writers and artists, his magnificent collections went to various museums in the two capitals, Petrograd and Moscow.

Objects of art and historical monuments were precious but of lesser moment to him than the men who understood, appreciated, made use of, and were engaged in creating and transmitting these precious things to future generations, and who, he hoped, might ultimately redeem the masses from their dark destructiveness and anarchy, and Russia from its "Asiatic backwardness."

Were it not for the magnificent scope and imagination with which Gorky went about his self-imposed tasks, few indeed of the intelligentsia would have survived those hard years. Hunger, cold, exhaustion from unsuitable labor, misprision by the new rulers of the intellectuals and their concerns—these enemies were everywhere. Among those who died of starvation even as Gorky was setting up the apparatus for their physical and spiritual sustenance were such luminaries of Russian scholarship as Professor Gezekhus, Assistant Rector of the Petersburg Technological Institute and a noted authority on molecular and acoustical physics (his work on the rubber molecule is still useful in the present day) ; Professor Brandt, authority on Slavistics; Professor

Batiushkov, authority on Gothic, Old High German, and Romanic languages and literatures; Professors Kosorolov of the Academy of Medicine, Khvostov of the University of Moscow, Blauberg of Odessa, the mathematician Lyapunov, who committed suicide because he saw no opportunity of continuing his work—a grim roll which could be enlarged indefinitely.[11]

The number of brain workers who perished during the early years of the revolution "exceeded by five or six times the number of citizens from the average citizenry. . . . There has been a staggering number of known deaths among Academicians [Members of the Academy of Sciences] from lack of nourishment and physical overexertion."[12]

The basic wealth of the country [Gorky wrote in anguish] consists of the amount of brains, the number of intellectual forces nurtured and accumulated by the nation. . . . It is of the utmost importance that the people possess a sufficient quantity of scientific workers, and that the lives of these men be not wasted senselessly. . . . If we compel a skilled metal engraver to clean cesspools, a goldsmith to forge anchors, a chemist to dig ditches, we are guilty not only of stupidity but of a crime. . . . We must realize that the labor of a scholar is the possession of all mankind, and that science is the realm of the highest disinterestedness. Workers in the fields of learning and science must be valued as the nation's most productive and most precious energy, and we must create such conditions as will facilitate in every way the growth of this energy. The premature breakdown or death of a scholar is an enormous loss for the country; this should be particularly clear to a workers' government. . . . Herewith is a list of scholars who have died within the last few months. . . . If this process of dying out of scholars should continue at such a speed,

---

[11] Another measure of the cultural decline is the fact that in 1913, under the last Tsar, over 34,000 titles were published, and this figure shrank to a mere 2,000 titles, mostly political or propagandistic, in 1920.

[12] Cited from a report of the Academy of Sciences in Kaun, *op cit.*, p. 486.

our country will be completely deprived of its brains. . . . In these hard days the life of a scientist is terrible physically, and tormenting morally for one who feels capable of moving mountains yet is deprived of the possibility of lifting a handful of sand. When such disgraceful things as lack of light for work, as cold and hunger, stand in the way of a great scientific discovery which might enrich the country and give happiness to millions, then it is criminal. . . .

Put that way, Lenin could agree. With the support of the man whose word was law in the Russia of the "proletarian dictatorship," and with unstinting aid from the Commissar of Education, Lunacharsky, Gorky hit upon a striking complex of solutions for the problem of conserving Russian culture. With the initiative and organizing genius of an Ignat Gordeyev—the merchant prince whom Gorky had portrayed so admiringly in his novel on the merchants of the Volga—the self-appointed Curator of Culture set up a veritable chain of cultural and literary enterprises that any merchant prince might envy. He became a big business man in the field of culture, a patron of all the arts and a protector of all who practised them, an impresario for theater and concert hall, a publisher with many and diverse publishing houses under his direction, the chairman of a Commission for the Improvement of the Life of Intellectuals and Scholars, an importuning fighter for increased rations, more fuel, more light, dwelling space, office space, laboratory space, an organizer of sheltering homes and institutions, a protector of those whose persons were in danger, a sponsor and patron wherever influence was necessary, the founder, director, and chairman of a whole galaxy of organizations for the encouragement of the activities and the saving of the lives and dignity of intellectuals.[13]

[13] The petitions, requests, protests, and appeals he addressed to Lenin on some of these matters occupy pp. 116–69 of *V. I. Lenin i A. M. Gorkii: Pisma*

To his Commission for the Protection of Art Objects, he added his Commission for the Improvement of the Living Conditions of Scholars, through which he succeeded in getting them warmer shelter; better light; an increase in rations (it took a special fight to get decent rations for "lower class," i.e. lesser lecturers, assistants, laboratory assistants, etc.) ; a Scholars' Home, with dormitories, rooms for reading and writing, lecture halls; access to sanatoria and summer resorts, and to special shops where they might buy some clothing, an item already even scarcer than food; a Writers' Home; a Home of the Arts, each similarly endowed; a publishing house of World Literature, with himself as director and a number of writers and scholars as advisers, staff members and translators; a publishing house for cheap editions of the Russian Classics; another for the publication of Contemporary Russian Writers; a journal for children; a Workers' University in the Uritsky Palace; a Commission for the Collection and Evaluation of Antiques and Antiquarian Books (some of these Gorky was willing to have sold abroad to raise money for the other activities) —indeed, so many enterprises, commissions, projects and institutions that it is impossible now to track them all down.

All of these enterprises were planned and set up as if for decades rather than to meet only an immediate emergency. World Literature had as its working program nothing less than the translation into Russian and publication of all the masterpieces of all lands and times. Another of his enterprises aimed at financing the dramatization of all the great novels of world literature and all the great moments of world

---

.... This does not include the innumerable telephone calls, the conversations on the occasions when Gorky went to Moscow to see Lenin on some special case, nor the irate notes of Gorky to Lenin which are still suppressed although sometimes Lenin's answers are given (see for example Lenin's answer to one of Gorky's still unpublished angry letters which appears in *Lenin*, Vol. XXXV, pp. 347–50).

history. Thus those who had been unable to sell original work for publication by an indigent and neglectful government, which was gradually taking over all stocks of paper, all printing presses, and all publishing, might at least live by translating into literary Russian the work of some writer they valued. The translations were paid for, however modestly, in "rations," in dwelling space, and in well-nigh worthless paper rubles. Many of the backlog of works thus translated still have not been printed; others are alive today as classics in their Russian translations. From the Committee on Historical Plays very little emerged in the way of actable dramas, but, like the other enterprises, it served to save the lives and the dignity of some intellectuals in those lean years.

Gorky presided over every commission, watched over every enterprise, conducted himself with modesty and decency —and astonishing knowledge—even when presiding over meetings of scholarly and scientific bodies. This self-taught vagrant who had made all knowledge his province and had a genuine reverence for all that men knew and thought and wrote, amazed and delighted the scholars whose meetings he chaired. All his unquenchable and unsystematic thirst for knowledge in all fields now seemed to fit him for the task he had assumed as the Curator of all the varied and multiple realms of culture.

Evgenii Zamyatin writes of this many-sided entrepreneur:

In a capital where there was not even bread, light, streetcars, in an atmosphere of catastrophe and ruin—these enterprises seemed at best fantasies of utopia. But Gorky believed in them ("one must believe") —and with his faith was able to infect the sceptical citizens of Petersburg. Learned academicians, poets, professors, translaters, dramatists, began to work in the institutions created by Gorky, becoming ever more absorbed in them. . . . Everywhere, Gorky was the permanent chairman. . . . More than once I asked myself in wonder: how many hours are there in this

man's day? . . . The miraculous medicine sustaining him in his
illness (tuberculosis) and his endless labors was . . . his faith.[14]

These are the words of one whom Gorky twice saved from
death—once from starvation, a second time when Stalin was
already settling old scores, but was persuaded by the Curator
to let Zamyatin go abroad, where he finished out his life in
lonely exile, maintaining to the end that "the world lives
only through heretics." The same kind of testimony to Gorky's care comes from countless writers who survived inside
Russia to become, for better or for worse, important figures
in the history of Soviet letters.

For better, surely, in the case of Kornei Chukovsky now in
his middle eighties, prisoner and deportee under the last
Tsar for his editorship of a political-satirical journal, transla-
tor of Walt Whitman and Shakespeare and many other An-
glo-Saxon writers into Russian, winner of an honorary degree of Doctor of Letters from Oxford and a Lenin Prize
from his own land, admired artist in a half-dozen genres, a
writer with one or more books in almost every Russian
home, beloved by millions of his countrymen for the bright-
ness he brought into their childhood by his humorous and
poetic fairy tales and verses for children, regarded with affection by his colleagues for the moral courage and sustained
imagination he has shown through all the vicissitudes of
machine-made five-year-plan literature and totalitarian literary dictatorship. He was saved for this long and fruitful life
by Gorky's intervention and, in his memoirs, remembers still
with gratitude the Allied Gorky Enterprises that enabled
him and so many of his generation to survive:

He not only presided over all our "Commissions" [writes
Chukovsky], but took upon his shoulders all our troubles and our
needs. . . . If one of us had a baby born, Gorky obtained a

[14] E. Zamyatin, *Litsa* (New York, 1955) , p. 90.

nipple, if one fell sick of typhus, he got him a place in a hospital
. . . if one desired to go to the country for a while, he wrote
letters to various institutions asking for permits. . . . Gorky
wrote neither stories nor novels, only these endless letters. . . .
Once a poetess called on him. After she left he remarked: "Only
the devil can understand them! No firewood, no light, no bread,
yet they go on as if everything were as usual . . . !" The poetess
had given birth to a child. . . . She got a permit: Milkwoman
So-and-So is hereby authorized to deliver milk to the wife of
Maxim Gorky, [Citizeness] So-and-So, and her name followed.
Another woman . . . Gorky put down as "my sister."

Thus did the man who once had so much trouble in New
York because of a woman not his wife, acquire wives, sisters,
daughters, and sons. These members of his enlarged family,
this host of protegés, some of them men and women unknown to him and not engaged in artistic pursuits, came to
him as a court of last resort.

They came [writes the poet Khodasevich] to ask intervention
on behalf of those who had been arrested. . . . to ask for rations,
rooms, clothes, medicines, fats, railway tickets, travel orders and
permits, tobacco, writing paper, ink, false teeth for the old and
milk for the newborn—whatever could not be obtained without
patronage.

Chukovsky sums it up for himself and all the others in
these words: "If we survived those breadless, typhus-filled
years, we owe it in large measure to our 'kinship' with
Maxim Gorky, to whom all of us became his 'family.' "[15]

[15] Chukovsky tells the story of Gorky's labors to save the lives of writers in
his Repin, Gorkii, Mayakovsky, Bryusov. Vospominaniya (Moscow, 1940),
and at greater length in Sovremenniki (Moscow, 1962), pp. 327–30. Though
Gorky had sacrificed his own profession as writer to this work of saving the
lives of the intelligentsia, Chukovsky estimates that "if we were to collect from
all institutions all the letters in which Gorky interceded at that time for
Russian writers, we would have at least six [additional] volumes of his prose."
Ibid., p. 327. He gives also the names of starving scholars in non-literary fields
who were sustained by their work in the Gorky Institute of World Literature,

The prose of even so plodding a party hack as Kornelii Zelinskii quickens when he pays his tribute to the heroic role played by Gorky in the preservation of Russian culture during the years between 1918 and 1920:

It would not be wrong to say that not a single significant beginning of a cultural nature, and more especially nothing connected with the creative intelligentsia in those years, took place without the close participation of Gorky. Gorky was the unofficial "president" of the entire intelligentsia, suffering with them and intervening for them with Lenin on all their concerns. . . . Gorky helped in the organizing of the Union of Writers and their Court of Honor [grievance committee], and the Union of Poets, and the Home of the Arts, and the Writers' Home, helped publishers, writers, scholars, helped every one he could in everything he could: with paper, advice, money, the fixing of academic rations, even with the simple matter of shoes. . . . In the editorial work alone of "World Literature" eighty writers and scholars were engaged. . . . Under his editorship some 120 works were published. . . . Writers were sustained both physically and spiritually. . . . In those years [he] mobilized and put to useful work almost all the forces of the prerevolutionary intelligentsia, and not only that, he was also the father and older friend of the writers of the new Soviet generation just beginning. . . .[16]

---

where they became advisers on the selection of classics for translation from whatever languages they knew.

[16] Kornelii Zelinskii, *Na rubezhe dvukh epokh: Literaturnye vstrechi, 1917–1920 godov* (*On the Border Between Two Epochs: Literary Encounters of the Years 1917–1920*), (Moscow, 1960), pp. 287–93.

CHAPTER VIII

Curator of Russian Culture
II: Justice for Grand Dukes and Poets

Lenin soon realized the usefulness of Gorky's enterprises, and the propaganda value for his regime that inhered in making the Curator's vast plans known abroad. Like an oriental potentate, Lenin had the power to cut through intervening channels, issue commands, direct the appropriation of funds, seize buildings, printing plants and paper stocks, transfer printers from plant to plant, and, in general, approve the petitions of this court favorite. Yet he was irritated, too, by Gorky's interference with the terror which seemed so necessary to him for the remaking of Russia according to his blueprint, and angry and hostile when Gorky asked for the right to reestablish his own paper, *Novaya Zhizn*. He was profoundly annoyed by the endless stream of protests and petitions on behalf of scholars, poets, grand dukes, and nameless individuals who meant something only to some mother or wife who had managed to touch Gorky's heart.

I troubled Lenin very often with all sorts of requests [Gorky was to remember later], and at times I felt that my pleas for people aroused in him a certain pity for me, even contempt. He would ask me: "Doesn't it occur to you that you are busying yourself with nonsense, with trifles?"

But I was doing what seemed to me to be necessary, and the ill-tempered and angry looks of a man who knew the number of the proletariat's enemies did not stop me. He would shake his head pityingly and say: "You are compromising yourself in the eyes of the workingmen and the comrades."

I pointed out that the comrades, and the workingmen, being in a state of anger and irritation, often treated liberty and the lives of valuable individuals too lightly and in too "simple" a manner. . . . This not only compromised . . . the revolution by superfluous and often absurd cruelty . . . it repelled many from aiding it. . . .

And yet I do not recall an instance when Ilyich refused a request of mine. [Gorky's memory had become charitable at the moment of Lenin's death.] If it happened, indeed, that my pleas were not granted, it was not his fault but the fault of those damned "mechanical shortcomings" from which the machine of the Russian state has always suffered in abundance. And we must also allow for some one else's malicious unwillingness to alleviate the fate of human beings, or save their lives. Vengeance and malice often act, too, by inertia. And then there are of course petty, psychically unhealthy people with a morbid thirst for the enjoyment of the suffering of their fellow men.

Gorky was thinking particularly of Zinoviev, with whom he had to deal as the boss of Petrograd, and of those specialists in sadistic cruelty that Dzerzhinsky himself was to find enlisting in excessive numbers in his Cheka.

Lenin lost his temper at times and flew into a rage at his Curator's endless interference with the built-in cruelties of his ruthless regime. "Dictatorship [he had declared after two years in power] is a harsh and bloody word." And for the soft-hearted, of whom Gorky was one, Lenin defined the term with beautiful simplicity:

The scientific concept of dictatorship means nothing more nor less than unlimited power resting directly on force, not restrained by anything, not restricted by any laws nor any absolute rules. Nothing else but that.[1]

---

[1] *Lenin,* Vol. XXXI, p. 326.

Still the artist, who could shed tears on the pages of his own manuscript when he was describing the sufferings of a fellow creature, persisted in his appeals to justice, mercy, compassion, to those very rules, moral and juridical laws, and customary traditions of humanity, from the restraints of which Lenin's "scientific definition" of total power and dictatorship were intended to free him. "You are wasting your time on trifles," Lenin would protest to him again and again. "This is only one lad [or only one bourgeois intellectual], and there is a revolution going on. Do you understand what a revolution is?" Gorky understood only too well, wherefore he did not cease to cry for the revolution to be just, merciful, considerate of individual life. Sometimes the two disagreed so hotly that it came, as Gorky told Alexander Kaun, "to shouting and banging on the table, with our faces flushed." How could these two men help but clash with each other when one of them believed in the sacredness and worth of each individual human life, and the other found it possible, as totalitarianism does, to condemn entire classes and categories of men not for individual actions but for their economic or hereditary blood guilt, their having been born into a family, a category or a class? Yet unlike Joseph Stalin who was to succeed him, Lenin had not entirely rid himself of the impedimenta of the humane tradition of the nineteenth-century intelligentsia, so that though often he lost his temper, perhaps just as often Gorky succeeded in touching some secret spring in his heart, and, to "humor" the petitioner, the dictator would unexpectedly yield.

Undoubtedly, the case that taxed Lenin's patience most sorely was that of the Grand Dukes whose wives came to Gorky's home in tears and whose guilt consisted exclusively in their having been born Great Princes of the House of Romanov, though personally they had abstained from doing anything in word or deed against the new regime. For the sake of the blood-taint of the name they bore, the Grand Dukes Pavel Alexandrovich, Georgii Mikhailovich, and Nikolai Mikhailovich were condemned to die. Only the first of them had an aggravating act charged against him: to wit, when he entered a theater—to his own embarrassment—the audience had recognized him and applauded. Under Nicholas, he had been Honorary Chairman of the Russian Society for the Protection of the Health of the People. Grand Duke Nikolai Mikhailovich was a member of the old Russian intelligentsia as a historian and Chairman of the Imperial Geographical and Historical Society. To Gorky, men born in the House of Romanov were also human, individual beings entitled to be judged by their acts, not their blood and name. When their wives came to him weeping, he got on the phone to argue their cases with Lenin, then made the wearying trip from Petrograd to Moscow to extract Lenin's signature on a document that would stay the execution and release the prisoners into Gorky's charge for appearance when summoned. What followed has been recorded by the wife of Dr. Manukhin,[2] a physician who had intervened on Gorky's behalf under the Tsar and now did the same for prisoners of the new regime.

I hastened to the station [Gorky told Dr. Manukhin] with the paper signed by Lenin, hurrying to catch that evening's train to Petrograd. On the platform I picked up an evening paper. . . .

[2] In the spring of 1901 Maxim Gorky was arrested in Nizhni Novgorod for such minor offenses as permitting meetings in his home, whereupon Tolstoy wrote on his behalf to Prince P. D. Svyatapolk-Mirsky, Deputy Minister of the Interior, and Prince P. A. Oldenburgsky, a brother-in-law of the Tsar, and within a month Gorky was released. He was arrested again in 1906 for more definitely political offenses connected with raising money for Father Gapon. On this occasion he was imprisoned in the Peter-Paul fortress, but under such conditions that he was able to write a play in prison (*The Children of the Sun*). Many foreign and Russian notables intervened on his behalf, and a number of doctors wrote concerning the condition of his lungs, whereupon he was permitted to go to the Crimea for his health and then to leave Russia for Italy.

ROMANOVS SHOT! I froze. I boarded the train, and remember nothing that followed. When I came to in the middle of the night, I was alone in an empty railway car on a siding in Klin.[3]

Had Zinoviev and the Petrograd Cheka acted on their own after learning that Gorky was returning with a reprieve? Had Lenin suggested that he was not too pleased with the document Gorky had managed to get him to sign? In any case, Gorky exonerated Lenin of responsibility.

Among the men whom the champion of simple justice succeeded in rescuing were two writers who fitted ill into the formulae of "the proletarian dictatorship." One was the pro-peasant novelist Ivan Volnyi. His pseudonym, *Volnyi,* is the Russian word for *free,* bespeaking a spirit that had little in common with Bolshevism. Before the revolution he was a member of a terrorist detachment of the Socialist Revolutionary Party. Like many another young writer, he was a friend and protegé of Maxim Gorky. In 1919 he told his patron that he was eager to go to some remote and quiet village to do his writing close to the peasants he idealized. His mentor, in a vein familiar to us, warned of the cruelty of the peasants, their contempt for men who work with quill and ink, and the crudeness of the petty bosses he would find in a remote village; but Volnyi could not be dissuaded. Before long the Narodnik writer found himself in a village jail with his papers and manuscripts confiscated, and his life itself in danger. To his protector he sent a cry for help, whereupon Gorky secured two telegrams from Lenin. The first went to the officials of the Archangelsk region:

> The writer, Ivan Volnyi, has been arrested. Gorky, his comrade, asks earnestly for the greatest care and objectivity in investigating him. Can he not be freed under close watch? Wire.

[3] Cited in David Shub, "Maksim Gorkii i kommunisticheskaiia diktatura," *Mosty* (Munich), No. 1, 1958, p. 243.

And two days later, Lenin wired to the tireless protector of young writers:

The Chairman of the Orlov Investigation Commission Chuzhinev wires me that Ivan Volnyi has been freed provisionally until the case is clarified.

Yet even the omnipotent name of Lenin was unable to restore to Volnyi the manuscript he had been working on, or his papers and books. A novel, a "chronicle," and a series of short stories had been destroyed by the village Cheka critic as of no literary value. The biography of Volnyi in the *Bolshaya Sovetskaya Entsiklopediia* is silent on this troubled page in the writer's life, but by way of recompense it tells us that in 1927 he began to repent his pro-peasant views and, in 1930, "adopted a new attitude toward the peasantry," enlisting in Stalin's great drive to reorganize the villages into compulsory collective farms. Whether he returned to the village as one of Stalin's scourges, or whether what he saw there shocked him as it did so many other idealistic young Communists, we shall never know, for he died in a remote village within the year.[4]

Another of the successes of this self-appointed court of appeals was the case of the writer Khodasevich. Vladislav Khodasevich was a poet whose spirit had not been made to fit either the prison yard of the League of Proletarian Writers (RAPP) or the straitjacket of "Socialist Realism." A mannerist, a mystic, a master of subtle poetic wit in the eighteenth-century sense of that term, he would have had no chance to write and be published in Russia had not his life and his talents been protected by Gorky's friendship and by the latter's conviction that Khodasevich was the greatest of living

---

[4] Volnyi's real name was Ivan Yegorovich Vladimirov. The *Entsiklopediia* lists him under yet another of his pen-names, I. V. Volnov. (*Bolshaia Sovietskaia Entsiklopediia,* 2d edition, 1951, Vol. IX, p. 61.)

Russian poets. The judgment is debatable, but the young poet's talents were undeniably large. When Gorky appealed to Lenin on his behalf, the latter did not pretend to be a judge of poetry, preferring to take Gorky's word that his protegé was a genius. Gorky tried to protect him, and give him a chance to write, by appointing him head of the Moscow Section of the Institute of World Literature, a sinecure which would leave him time to write undisturbed since Gorky handled the Institute's affairs single-handed from Petrograd. But the appointment did not save the poet from conscription and an order that he be sent at once to the front to fight in the Civil War. Gorky went straight to Lenin to plead that Khodasevich would be more valuable wielding a pen than a sword. Lenin had the call-up revoked; this time, for greater security, Gorky made the poet part of his large household, where he could be kept under the older writer's protective eye. In time he got Khodasevich permission to go abroad to work with him as co-editor of a magazine to be called *Beseda,* which in this context might be translated as *Dialogue,* since Gorky was planning it as a magazine in which both emigré and Soviet writers might be published and speak to each other through their work. To Khodasevich we owe some interesting reminiscences concerning Gorky, the last and ablest published in 1939, the year of the poet's death.[5]

The adoption of a poet as a member of his own household was a frequent protective device, for in Russia as in Italy, in good seasons and in bad, the great writer's home was always swarming with guests and hangers on. If someone arrived at the dinner hour, he was fed; if he stayed on, he was given a

---

[5] V. F. Khodasevich, *Nekropol: Vospominaniya* (Brussels, 1939) , pp. 228–77. Despite angry protests from Gorky, Lenin would not permit the dialogue. Not one writer from inside the Soviet Union was permitted to send *Beseda* a contribution, and not one copy of *Beseda* was permitted to enter Russia. On this see Chapter VII.

room—or a corner of a room—and something to sleep on. Unless he actually disturbed the writer's work, no one was ever asked when he expected to leave. Writers and would-be writers, actors and playwrights, musicians and singers, a troop of secretaries—one or more of whom was always a member of the Cheka delegated to report on his activities—visitors and vagrants elegant and poor, in Italy Russians abroad longing for a bit of Russia, in Russia anyone who was in danger or in need, all found an open house. Gorky told his biographer, Kaun:

> There were always twenty-five to thirty people at our table in Petrograd. One evening a squad of soldiers broke in "searching for bombs." They were hungry, so were we. But at eight that night a chap had brought us a wonderful gift: potatoes, beets, three lake whitefish, a goodly slab of bacon. At midnight . . . our cook brought in the whole business in a gigantic pan. We had been wrangling with the soldiers over the silly matter of looking for bombs in my residence. . . . Their eyes popped out, their mouths drooled. "Sit down boys." And they did. . . .[6]

No doubt the strangest member of his great patriarchal household was yet another Grand Duke, Gavriil Konstantinovich Romanov, who moved in one day with his wife, Antonina Rafailovna Nesterovskaya, who was a former ballet dancer, her maid, and her bulldog. Since the bulldog did not seem to like the bohemian and proletarian guests, he had to be kept tied up in a blanket to prevent him from actively showing his displeasure. Grand Duke Gavriil, like all the members of the Romanov family, was in danger of death for blood-guilt. In addition, he was gravely ill and was attended by Gorky's own physician and friend, Dr. Manukhin, who persuaded Gorky to make his home the Grand Duke's hospital and refuge. Gorky remembered, too, that Gavriil's father,

---

[6] Kaun, *op. cit.*, 495.

Konstantin Konstantinovitch Romanov, had been President of the Russian Academy of Sciences in 1902 when Gorky was elected to membership (an election vetoed by Nicholas II), and that, under the pen-name *K. R.,* Grand Duke Konstantin had shown himself to be a talented poet. Gorky made his ailing son welcome in his home. Taught by his experience with the other three Grand Dukes, whom Zinoviev had had killed while their protector was journeying with a reprieve written in Lenin's hand, the writer went straight to Zinoviev, whom he detested but knew how to bribe with such things as signed articles in *Petrogradskaya Pravda.* His problem was to write something that would please and flatter Zinoviev without belying his own convictions. In another connection we shall examine one of these *wergild* articles (see Chapter IX).

Gavriil Konstantinovich was suffering from tuberculosis. Somehow, Gorky prevailed upon Zinoviev to issue a permit for the patient to go to Finland for treatment. But of course this was the kind of thing that Zinoviev would immediately report to Lenin, either in the line of duty or as a juicy bit of gossip. "In the illness of a Romanov I do not believe," wired Lenin. "I forbid the journey."

Lenin's displeasure did not cause the poet from the lower depths to give up his royal guest. At Gorky's table the Romanov couple met such Bolshevik notables as Lunacharsky and Stasova. Inevitably, at times arguments took place, so that in the end the Romanovs were able to converse only with their host, his actress wife Andreeva, and the former Court favorite, the great singer Shalyapin. After a while Gorky made a new appeal to Zinoviev, this time securing from the boss of Petrograd an exit permit, a travel order, and even some spending money for the journey of his princely guest. On November 11, 1918, without Lenin's being apprised, Gavriil Konstantinovich Romanov, his wife, her maid, and her bulldog, all crossed the frontier into Finland, where in a sanatorium the Grand Duke's illness was arrested. He lived for another twenty years and told the story of how Gorky saved his life in memoirs entitled *V Mramornom Dvortse (In a Marble Palace)*, New York, 1955. To have saved the life of even one Grand Duke out of four was an astonishing feat, a feat such as only Gorky could contemplate and only he could have brought off. But Lenin was annoyed, for he could not get it out of his head that every Romanov deserved to die because he was a Romanov and therefore might hypothetically serve as a rallying point of counterrevolution.

CHAPTER IX

Curator of Russian Culture
III: The Death of Two Poets

Early in 1921, the breach between Lenin and Gorky began to widen again, and the frail bridge threatened to fall once more into the abyss. Gorky's alienation was occasioned by two acts of grave injustice on Lenin's part, and the loss of the lives of two poets for whom Gorky was interceding.

The first injustice was Zinoviev's treatment, with Lenin's and Trotsky's full support, of protests by the workingmen of Petrograd and the sailors of Kronstadt. Since the Civil War had ended in victory for the Bolsheviks, the sailors of Kronstadt (with whose active support Lenin had seized power), and the workingmen of the capital and the peasants of all Russia (with whose passive support he had maintained himself in power) felt it was high time at last for Lenin to lighten their hard lot and keep some of the promises he had made them on his way to power. The wages of the industrial workers were far below a living minimum—their unrest was being held down by Trotsky's plan for the conscription of released Red Army soldiers as a conscript "labor army." Workingmen travelling to the country to supplement their meager rations by bartering or buying needed food from the peasants were treated by Lenin's *Cheka* as "bagmen" guilty of the crime of "speculation." The promised Constituent Assembly had been dispersed by force of arms. The Soviets that were to have received "all power" had been gutted of any semblance of democracy by the outlawing of all other democratic and socialist parties, and all power had passed into the hands of the Bolshevik Party and its leaders. Even in the party itself discontent on these scores was grave, with Lenin's old wartime lieutenants, Shlyapnikov and Kollontay, leading a "Workers' Opposition." When strikes broke out in Petrograd and the sailors of Kronstadt made modest demands for free elections to the Soviets and freedom of trade in the necessities of life between city and country, the entire population of the Kronstadt naval base, including garrison, sailors, and the Kronstadt Communists, unanimously supported this petition for an alleviation of their hard life. Lenin began to reexamine the collision course on which he had embarked with his false economic ukases. But first Zinoviev, backed by Lenin and Trotsky and the majority of the top officialdom then in session in the Tenth Congress of their Party, determined to "teach the masses a lesson" and put an end to the "petty-bourgeois spontaneity" (i.e. the self-activity, elemental force, and sense of freedom) which Lenin declared to be "more terrible than all the Denikins, Kolchaks, and Yudeniches put together."[1] The party congress under Lenin's leadership pronounced this simple petition and protest to be a "rebellion," engineered as a "White Guard plot" and inspired and backed by a "foreign power." The petitioners were called mutineers, and branded "Denikin's allies, and pawns in Denikin's game." While Lenin did not think it wise to point out that the Workers' Opposition within the Communist Party was making demands similar to those of the workingmen of Petrograd and the sailors of Kronstadt, to the Congress he said ominously, "Armies in retreat are accustomed to turn machine guns on the few

---

[1] *Lenin*, Vol. XXVII, pp. 303–04; Vol. XXX, pp. 155, 339. Denikin, Kolchak, and Yudenich were the leading generals of the White Armies that had just been defeated in the Civil War.

voices of panic." In place of machine guns, he put through a measure prohibiting the formation of groupings within the party under penalty of expulsion. Thus the last vent for public discussion was plugged.

By acts and pronouncements of Zinoviev and Lenin, a rising was deliberately provoked at Kronstadt. On March 2 the fortress and its garrison were declared to be engaged in a "White Guard mutiny." Sixteen days later it was all over, the movement having been completely crushed after a fierce and bloody attack on the Fortress of Kronstadt over the ice of the frozen Gulf of Finland by specially picked Red Army troops from the Far East, Red officers and officer candidates, led by some three hundred delegates from the Congress itself, directed by War Commissar Trotsky and Army Commander Tukhachevsky. Wounded prisoners of war were butchered in the streets of Kronstadt and on Anchor Square. Those who survived filled the prisons and the far northern concentration camp on Solovetsky Island in the Arctic Circle. A number of additional sailors were shot by the Cheka a few months later.[2]

This is not the place to tell this grim story. Here it suffices to note that Lenin himself acknowledged to the Congress that the "White Guard conspiracy" charge was a legend.[3] Maxim Gorky sought to put the main blame not on Lenin but on Zinoviev, yet the gulf between the two friends widened perceptibly as a result of this injustice. Gorky even hid

[2] See pp. 121–32 for an account of the "Tagantsev Conspiracy."

[3] Lenin told the Tenth Congress, then in session: "The experience of Kronstadt [shows] that there they do not want the White Guard, nor do they want our rule—and there is no third. . . ." *Lenin,* Vol. XXXII, p. 204. Bukharin, less cynical than Lenin, told the Third Congress of the Comintern, "For the sake of the idea, for the sake of our task, we were forced to repress the revolt of our erring brothers. We cannot look upon the Kronstadt sailors as our enemies. We love them as our true brothers, our own flesh and blood. . . ." For a well documented account of the Kronstadt affair see George Katkov, *The Kronstadt Rising,* St. Antony's Papers, No. 6 (New York, 1959), pp. 9–74.

fugitive sailors in his home while he besieged Lenin with petitions for their exoneration.

The other case of injustice touched Gorky more closely, for it was Lenin himself who got Gorky mixed up in it. The original pact between the two men, made at Lenin's bedside when he was recovering from the pistol wound in his neck, carried with it the understanding that Gorky would use his influence with the Russian intelligentsia to get them to cooperate with the Bolshevik regime. The poet had tried on more than one occasion to carry out his promise to the politician, but the nature of the dictatorship did not make it easy. Thus in October 1920, Gorky visited his old friend Kuskova, to propose that she and her husband, the economist Prokopovich, call together representatives of the old Russian intelligentsia for a talk with the dictator. For several days intellectuals of various tendencies met in little groups to consider this novel invitation, then all of them, with only two unimportant exceptions, decided to decline the honor. Some feared reprisals for their disrespectful temerity toward the all-powerful one, yet all of them were firm in their answer. Here is Kuskova's explanation to Gorky of their motives:

We, the intelligentsia, are prisoners of the dictatorship; we have no press, no organizations, no open meetings, nor in general any means of expressing our views and testing them as to their acceptance by the people of our country. Since we are bound and silenced, we cannot represent any interest even with the representatives of the Soviet power. And under these conditions, with the intellectuals aware of their real helplessness, it is quite useless to have talks with those who have created and maintain such a situation.[4]

[4] Cited from E. Kuskova, "Mesyats 'Soglashatelstva'" (Month of "Reconciliation"), *Volya Rossii* (Prague), 1928. Her article was printed in three parts in Nos. 3, 4, and 5, pp. 50–69, 43–61, 58–78. The account of the Public Famine Relief Committee which follows is drawn principally from this series.

Lenin seemed to comprehend this dignified stand, showing no resentment at their refusal to meet with him, while Gorky, who understood and agreed with the voiceless intellectuals, simply gave up all attempts to arrange a meeting. However, as famine spread through the land during the winter and spring of 1921 and these public figures learned from comrades in the famine area how frightful things were, they met on their own initiative to offer their services for famine relief to Lenin's government as they had previously to the Tsar's. It was Kuskova and Prokopovich who called their friends together to hear a report from the Volga famine region, and it was Kuskova who spoke to Gorky of their readiness to serve. Gorky hastened to Lenin.

Hitherto the Bolshevik leader had been adamant in his insistence that there be no organization of any kind independent of the party and the state. The Tsar's government too had been distrustful of the self-activity of such public figures, but, since it was less totalitarian in its ambitions, it had been far less severe in its prohibition of independent public life.

Lenin reflected. The emergency was grave. His government he knew—thanks to its subversive activities and openly inflammatory manifestoes to the workingmen of other lands—enjoyed neither credit sufficient to receive large supplies from abroad nor trust to distribute them impartially to the needy. Here were names he could use, people known and trusted abroad, who could appeal alike to governments, public figures, and charitable organizations, for massive help. There was danger, to be sure, that they would make themselves known again and popular in the land, and might accustom themselves to meeting together and discussing public affairs. Yet the need was extreme: millions were fated to perish even if massive relief came. And what country would give help to him and to the regime he had set up to win the world? The political question involved was to Lenin an old one: *Kto kogo? Who uses whom?* To him this question was the essence of all politics in every alliance. The trump cards of power and press and police and officials and transport were all in his hands. The game was worth trying.

Gorky received encouragement to take part in a famine relief committee of public figures, with a suitable admixture of Communist leaders, under the domination of the Communist Fraction of the committee.

On July 2, the graveyard stillness of public life under the Bolsheviks was broken by a startling news note in *Izvestia* that some well known public figures were about to set up a nongovernmental famine relief committee. A few days later, none other than Lev Borisovich Kamenev, Chairman of the Moscow Soviet and Deputy Chairman of the Council of People's Commissars, telephoned citizen Prokopovich to ask him to call together some prominent public figures. Kamenev indicated his own willingness to serve on the Famine Relief Committee and act as its chairman, a willingness which was tantamount to a designation. On July 21, people read with wonder the names of public figures long in oblivion: an All-Russian Famine Relief Committee of some ten or so Communist officials of high rank and some fifty-odd public figures from the suppressed and forgotten past.

Among the Communists were Kamenev as Chairman; Rykov, Lenin's first deputy on the Council of Commissars, as Vice-Chairman; Krassin, Commissar of Trade; Lunacharsky, Commissar of Education; Semashko, Commissar of Health; Teodorovich, Commissar of Agriculture; Shlyapnikov, Commissar of Labor; Litvinov, representing the Commissariat of Foreign Affairs; and a few lesser luminaries of the new Communist ruling circles.

The list of noncommunist public figures was no less impressive. There were such well known writers as Koro-

lenko, Gorky, and Boris Zaitsev, and such liberal and socialist political figures as Prokopovich, Kuskova, Kutler, and
Nikolai Mikhailovich Kishkin. Kishkin, a medical doctor
and Kadet leader who had served in the last days of the
Provisional Government, had been arrested in the last-ditch
defense of the Winter Palace, released, rearrested by the
Cheka in 1919, charged with participation in a conspiracy to
overthrow the dictatorship of Lenin and set up a democratic
government, and kept in prison until the beginning of 1921.
Now not only was he authorized to serve on the Famine
Relief Commission, but, though broken in health by his stay
in prison, he was to act as spokesman for the non-party public
figures, answering Chairman Kamenev's pledge of government support by a pledge on their part that the commission
would be nonpolitical in its relief and would subordinate
itself to the procedures and direction of the Red Cross. There
was Fedor Alexandrovich Golovin, whose name was well
known abroad because he had been chairman of the Second
Duma and had served in the Third Duma as well; during
the war he had been a leader of the Union of Towns, which,
in conjunction with the Union of Zemstvos, carried on under
Nicholas II the public's independent war and Red Cross
work; then he had become a commissar of the Provisional
Government, and though he was shortly to be thrown into
prison again, he would finish out his days working as a
specialist in various Soviet institutions. A name to conjure
with in appealing for foreign aid was that of Alexandra
Tolstoy, daughter of the world-renowed novelist. She had
already been in and out of several Soviet jails. She had spent
two months undergoing questioning in the dread prison of
the Cheka in the Lubyanka for having permitted friends to
use her quarters for a meeting, which she did not herself
attend, of the so-called "Tactical Center." She had been released until her trial and resulting condemnation to three

years of forced labor at the former Novospassky Monastery. After a few months she was released once more on the intervention of Bolshevik leader Alexandra Kollantay, backed by a petition of the peasants of her father's former estate; then jailed again for the crime of attending a lecture by her father's secretary, Bulgakov, which dealt with Lev Tolstoy's opposition to capital punishment. Released once more to take charge of the Tolstoy Museum in Yasnaya Polyana, she was now recruited as a leading figure in the Famine Relief Committee. Other prominent committee members included Sergei Bulgakov, who in his early years had been a Marxist and was to end his life as an Orthodox priest and teacher of theology; Yuzhin-Sumbatov, the actor and dramatist born of a noble Georgian family, who soon would be decorated as a "People's Artist"; Vera Figner, venerable terrorist and revolutionist of an earlier day, who had spent long years in prison until the Provisional Government released her in one of its first decrees freeing political prisoners of the old regime. There were cooperative leaders, former leaders in banking and finance, in medicine and health, and many other well known figures of the past who had become unpersons because the Communist monopoly press gave them no place to write, took no notice of their deeds or their dreams, nor of their existence. The secretary of the commission was S. A. Benkendorf, another name well known abroad because his father had been Russia's ambassador to England. The commission was allowed to adopt its own bylaws—a "constitution" Kuskova called it—to carry on elections by secret ballot, to issue a journal concerning famine conditions and its own relief activities, and to send a small committee abroad to appeal for help. It was as a member of the Famine Relief Committee that Maxim Gorky himself sent abroad a moving personal appeal for the help of "all honest persons."

From Gorky, Kuskova learned that from the outset among

the Communist leaders there were two tendencies or atti-
tudes toward the new committee: the "Kremlin tendency,"
which favored using the commission and for this purpose
giving it cautious leeway; and the "Lubyanka tendency"
(the Lubyanka was short for the headquarters and cellar
dungeons of the Cheka on Lubyanka Square), which, as the
Russian police and bureaucracy have always done, distrusted
any independent public activity. The first tendency felt it
was worth a calculated risk to get names of such standing to
use, and with their help perhaps get several million poods of
grain from abroad. To the "Lubyanka tendency," the whole
idea of a self-administering group even under Communist
domination seemed dangerous and under no circumstances
to be tolerated. What Gorky did not realize was that Lenin
himself was of two minds, and that Kremlin and Lubyanka
coexisted in his spirit.

A constitution [Kuskova was to write out of her experience in
serving under both Tsar and Commissars on such relief commit-
tees] for any non-state organization is intolerable to any autocracy, even when it does no harm to the ruling power. Autocracy is
organically unable to tolerate the most innocent freedom. And
therefore it is impossible to foresee where, when, and from what,
a conflict may break out. . . .[5]

The conflict came sooner than Kuskova expected. The
committee held two fruitful meetings under Kamenev's chair-
manship. He came on time, ruled the meetings courteously
and considerately. There were some minor differences over
such matters as whether Russians who had fled abroad would
be willing to help and should be approached for sympathy
and support (Krassin put his foot down on that: "There are
no Russians abroad, only traitors."). But generally everything went courteously and efficiently; the machinery for

5 Kuskova, *loc. cit.*, No. 5, p. 66.

gathering massive help from the only place from which it could come—from the "capitalist world"—began to move smoothly. Kuskova and Prokopovich were delegated to go abroad in search of help. Then the unexpected happened: Herbert Hoover cabled Maxim Gorky on behalf of the American Relief Administration in answer to Gorky's personal appeal:

I have read with great feeling your appeal to Americans for charitable assistance to the starving and sick people of Russia. . . . We are today caring for three and one-half million children in ten different countries, and would be willing to furnish necessary supplements of food, clothing and medical supplies to a million children in Russia as rapidly as organization could be effected.[6]

Hoover made a few necessary stipulations, all of which (with one exception) applied to all the countries the American Relief Administration had aided. The one additional demand was that Americans who had been arrested in Russia and were being kept in prison instead of being permitted to return home, should be released, so that all Americans could more easily be appealed to for generous help.

The other conditions, he telegraphed, "are identically the same as those that have been established in every one of the twenty-three countries where operations have been conducted." The government would have to state that there was need (Lenin so far had officially denied the very existence of a famine, a denial which made an appeal to the American people impossible) ; the representatives of the A.R.A. would have to have "full liberty to come and go . . . to organize local committees free from governmental interference . . . to receive the necessary facilities . . . to receive assurances that people thus helped would not lose their regular rations."

[6] See Plate XVII.

On its side [Hoover added] the Relief Administration is prepared as usual to make a free and frank undertaking:

FIRST. That it will . . . supply all children and invalids alike without regard to race, creed, or social status.

SECOND. That its representatives will engage in no political activities.

That settled it for Lenin. As Deputy Foreign Commissar Litvinov told Hoover, "Food is a weapon." The names on the Public Committee had done their work; the committee itself had been bypassed in a personal telegram to a single one of its members; the usefulness of the experiment had been exhausted; in Lenin's mind the Lubyanka tendency triumphed over the Kremlin tendency.

When the third meeting assembled at its customary hour, Chairman Kamenev was for the first time late, and all the other Communist notables strangely absent, too. A phone call got an embarrassed reply from Kamenev: something had delayed him and he could not be there on time. Even as this reply was being communicated to the assembled members, the platform filled with Chekists, fully armed. Other Chekists lined the walls, filled the doorways; "Comrade Cheka" was in the Chair. The Chekist chairman called out the names of Vera Figner, veteran revolutionist; of Lev Alexandrovich Tarasevich, a distinguished immunologist and microbiologist who after his death would have an Institute of Immunology named after him; of Yuzhin-Sumbatov, the well known actor who in 1923 would be made Director of the Maly Teatr; and of P. A. Sadyrin, the outstanding authority on and leader of the agricultural cooperative movement. These were told to leave the hall. Then the commander of the Cheka detachment, after making sure that such men as Gorky and Korolenko, whose arrest would have proved embarrassing, were not present, put all the others, including foreign newspapermen, into patrol wagons which took them to the dungeons of the Lubyanka. In prison they were treated with unusual courtesy, for Lubyanka inmates. Some were released in a few hours or a few days. But the leading figures were charged with conspiring against the state and secretly fomenting peasant uprisings in the famine areas and, without a hearing, were condemned by a Cheka tribunal to execution by firing squad. Those condemned to death included Prokopovich and Kuskova.

An influential person, whose name Kuskova preferred to leave unmentioned since, when she wrote of this, he was still alive and in the Soviet Union, went first to the head of the Cheka and then to Lenin to inquire concerning the crimes of the condemned. The Cheka leader responded:

You say that the Committee didn't take a single illegal step. That is true. But it was a center of attraction for all the so-called Russian "public." . . . This we could not permit. . . . When you put an unsprouted willow branch into water, it quickly begins to sprout. . . . With the same speed, the Russian "public" began to swell up as did the Committee and its influence. . . . The willow twig had to be thrown out of the water and stamped on.

And Lenin told the same person:

Did the Committee really commit all those crimes? Not at all! Nothing of the sort! We know perfectly well the loyalty of the conduct of all the members of the Committee. But it was necessary for us—for political reasons—to destroy it.[7]

Gorky was furious when he learned of Lenin's perfidy and the death sentences meted out to the people who had, on Lenin's assurance and his own request, formed the Committee. What he said to Lenin in the angry encounter that followed we will never know, for the famine was so serious and Hoover's message involved him so personally that he could not make any public utterance on the frameup. But to

[7] *Ibid.*, pp. 68, 76.

Kamenev he said: "You have turned me into an *agent provo-cateur*. This is the first time in my life that such a thing has happened to me." Lenin began to wonder whether it would not be better for Gorky to leave Russia "for his health." Clearly, his sense of justice was becoming a nuisance.

Fortunately, the sudden disappearance of so many public figures within a month after *Izvestia* had called attention to their existence and their humanitarian activities, did not pass unnoticed. Prominent public figures of other lands, trying to get in touch with them to offer help, learned that they had vanished into the dungeons of the Lubyanka. Both Herbert Hoover and Fridtjof Nansen, the most prominent European engaged in international relief activities, sent sharp protests to Lenin, whereupon, just as suddenly, Lenin had them released and deported from their native land. Kuskova and Prokopovich, and a little later, Bulgakov and a few others, had their death sentences commuted and were enabled to live out their lives in freedom—but far from the land they loved and had so faithfully served under the despotism of both Nicholas II and V. I. Lenin.

All of them lived out their lives first in Prague and then in Paris, except for Alexandra Tolstoy, who was refused the right to go abroad and, after a few days in jail, was put in charge once more of her father's papers and relics at Yasnaya Polyana. In 1929, friends managed to get her invited by a number of Japanese universities to lecture on her father's views. Lest a world scandal arise from a refusal to let her go to Japan, she was grudgingly granted a passport valid for three months. Once abroad, she never returned to her native land but went to America, where she published memoirs on her father (*Otets*), and in both English and Russian an autobiographical account of her life in the Soviet Union (*Probleski vo tme—Gleams of Light in the Dark*, translated into English under the title *I Worked for the Soviet*). In

America, on a farm in New Jersey, she carries on notable relief work for Russian refugees and aids them to get their bearings and integrate themselves into American life.

Bulgakov became a theologian of note and an orthodox priest, dying in Paris in 1944. Kuskova carried on a distinguished career as a publicist in the Russian colonies of Prague and Paris for over three decades. Her husband, Sergei Nikolaevich Prokopovich, achieved an international reputation as the economist who made pioneer studies of the gross national product of the Soviet Union.[8] He died in 1955, she in 1958. Their lives would not have lasted so long nor been so fruitful under the harsh rule of Lenin and Stalin, but all her life Kuskova continued wistfully to search the horizon for signs that the ways of the new rulers of Russia were becoming gentler, so that her people would suffer less and she might have a chance to return to her native land to serve them with dignity. Though she lived until 1958, the chance never came.

Gorky could not recall without tears the bitter year of the great famine. In 1925 in Italy, he told his biographer, Alexander Kaun:

> We hungered terribly. More than a hundred scholars died from lack of nourishment. You cannot realize what it means to starve for fats and sweets. With the first money from American relief we sent an expedition to Central Asia for fats and sweets. A case of dried peaches arrived. . . . There they stood—venerable men, scientists, international celebrities, trembling hands instinctively stretching out for the delicacies, eyes burning with greed. . . . I recall Professor Khvolson lecturing on Einstein, clinging with his hands to the lectern, swaying to and fro as if he were on a steamship on a stormy sea. . . . Sergei Oldenburg, Permanent Secretary of the Academy of Sciences, flaunting his felt boots. . . .

[8] Sergei Nikolaevich Prokopovich, *Narodnoe Khozyaistvo S.S.S.R.* (New York, 1952) , published in German and French in 1944.

Professor Simkevich, Rector of the University of Petrograd, huddled up in a corner over a bowl of gruel . . . devouring it avidly, eyes flitting about the room like those of a baby afraid lest some one take away its goody.[9]

Gorky told Kaun nothing of Lenin's perfidy in connection with the Public Famine Relief Committee. Nor did he allude to the fact that the men whose lives he had saved were from that "bourgeois intelligentsia" which Lenin had classified as "class enemies." Nor did he say he had been right and Lenin wrong in his basic belief that achievements in the arts, the growth of knowledge, and the development of science, are classless achievements valuable and precious to all mankind. *I told you so* was not a part of Gorky's lexicon.

Even in the midst of famine, the Curator of Culture still had to contend with official neglect and the ever-present danger of the firing squad. The death of two great Russian poets, one by neglect, the other by shooting, now filled Gorky's cup of bitterness to overflowing.

The first was the great symbolist poet Aleksandr Blok. His sensitive spirit had foreknown the breakdown of the old Russia for a full decade before the Tsar fell. In 1908 he "heard the breathless rush of the *troika* . . . in and out of the snowdrifts on the dead and desolate plain . . . bearing Russia at headlong speed to an unknown destination." He saw the coming revolution as the strokes of the peasant axe attempting to break through from the decaying old Russia into a new peasant kingdom. Sometimes he saw the peasant picking up a torch and setting fire to the old world while "God sends no rain and what there is, is burning." Publicly he wrote in January 1918, in "The Intelligentsia and the

[9] Kaun, *op. cit.*, p. 491. Oldenburg, Permanent Secretary of the Academy, was kept alive not by Academy stipend but because Gorky appointed him expert on Indian literature in the Institute of World Literature. On this see Chukovsky, *Sovremenniki*, p. 329.

Revolution," ". . . the duty of the artist is . . . to listen to the music in the wind-torn air. . . . See that everything becomes new, that our lying, dirty, tedious, discordant life becomes a just, clean, gay, beautiful life. . . ."

And in his diary:

This is the task of Russian culture: to direct this fire to that which should be burned; to transform the rioting of Stenka Razin and Yemelyan Pugachov into a harmonious wave of music; to set limits to destruction which will not weaken the force of the fire but will guide it aright. To organize the impetuous will, the lazy smoldering [resentment] that conceals latent violence, to send it into the darkest and vilest corners of the soul and there to flame—sky-high—to burn away the sly, lazy, servile flesh.[10]

Blok strove to welcome the revolution with an act of faith in an impending miracle. Perhaps indeed the flames would consume only what was evil, the axe destroy what was rotting, and the intelligentsia guide the untutored masses into the building of a new Russia, beautiful and pure. In January 1918, he looked out of his window as darkness deepened amidst the swirling snowstorm. In the snow his fantasy descried twelve rough and ragged Red Army men marching, burning, shooting, looting, avenging ancient wrongs, perpetrating new ones, marching on through blizzard and wind, through hatred and blood, destroying the old world, making perhaps the new. Through the swirling snow drifts his fantasy perceived:

With mist-white roses garlanded,
Jesus Christ marching at their head.[11]

[10] The above quotations and all those that follow are taken from the remarkable study of Aleksandr Blok and Nikolai Gumilev, in Vyacheslav Zavalishin, *Early Soviet Writers* (New York, 1958), pp. 5–22. The prose translations are by Mrs. Nicholas Vakar; the poetry translations, occasionally slightly modified by the author, are by Miss Valentine Snow.

[11] From the translation of Babette Deutsch and Avrahm Yarmolinsky.

He called the long poem with its wind-blown snow, its marching men, its bloody deeds, its rallying cries, its twelve ragged soldiers, and its twelve varied episodes, "The Twelve." Were these ragged, ruthless men the twelve disciples? Was the spirit that guided them Christ? or anti-Christ? Were they merely destroying?

Lock your doors and windows tight!
There are looters out tonight!
Burst the cellars—wine is free!
Tonight the rabble's on the spree.

Or were they also clearing the ground for something new and good?

As I worked on "The Twelve" [Blok wrote later], and for several days after, I kept hearing—I mean hearing literally with my ears—a great noise around me, a steady noise (perhaps it was the noise of the old world crumbling) .

The poem created a sensation. For a while the Bolsheviks thought they had found in this great master of verbal music and imagery their poet. But as he watched "the inner barbarians" at their cruel and destructive work, his hope gave way to disillusionment and despair.

Peace and freedom! [he cried in a speech on the anniversary of the death of Pushkin made in February, 1921] They are essential to the poet for the release of music. But peace and freedom are taken away also . . . the freedom of creation, the inner freedom. And the poet dies because there is nothing for him to breathe. Life has lost its meaning.

When he pronounced those words of challenge and despair, the poet's inability to breathe was at once physical and spiritual. Censorship, and the party's control of publication and printing, choked him. The hunger and heatless lodgings gave him rheumatic fever. His heart began to weaken; he found difficulty breathing. His spirit was sick with remorse and despair for having misread the meaning of the revolution. His only hope was to get permission to depart for a sanatorium in a sunnier, warmer, more opulent and less dictatorial land. What other land denied its citizens permission to go abroad for their health or recreation? Gorky had the Writers' Union adopt a petition asking for a visa for Blok. For six tedious, frightening months, he went from bureaucrat to bureaucrat, from office to office, for favorable action on that resolution. Winter turned to spring, then to summer; at last, on August 10, 1921, the permit came—one day too late. The great poet had died the night before.

Some two weeks later, on August 23 or 24, 1921, another great poet, Nikolai Stepanovich Gumilev, was shot by the Petrograd Cheka for "participation in the conspiracy of Tagantsev." He had been in prison only a few days, where he sat serenely reading Homer and the Gospels and writing verses, just as he had on shipboard and on the battlefields of the World War. There was no trial. No clear account of the so-called Tagantsev conspiracy has ever been published. A committee of intellectuals formed at the funeral of Blok went from prison to prison looking for the arrested poet. It consisted of S. F. Oldenburg, Permanent Secretary of the Academy, the literary critic A. L. Volynsky, the journalist N. M. Volkovyskii, and the writer Alexander Avdeevich Otsup. They had the endorsement of the Academy of Sciences, of the Institute of World Literature, and of Proletkult, to petition the Cheka to release Gumilev into their custody. The Academy of Sciences offered to guarantee his appearance when wanted for trial. At the same time, Maxim Gorky set out for Moscow to ask Lenin's intervention on behalf of one of Russia's greatest poets, who could do more for Russian culture as a poet than for the politics of the dictatorship as a victim of a firing squad. The Chairman of the Petrograd

Cheka, Bakaev, told the commission that Gumilev had been arrested for committing "a crime in the course of service at his official post." Oldenburg answered that the poet had no official post. Bakaev began to realize that influential people were intervening on behalf of his victim, both in Moscow and Petrograd. "At present," he said, "I can't tell you anything. Call me Wednesday. In any case, not a hair of Gumilev's head will fall." Before the date of the telephone call, Gumilev was dead.[12] Thus Maxim Gorky had to witness, within a period of less than a month, the loss by Russia of two of its greatest contemporary poets. Clearly the pact between Russia's dictator and the Curator of Russian Culture was breaking down, and both men realized it at the same moment.

Like the "conspiracy" of Kuskova, Prokopovich, and the Public Famine Relief Committee, the "Tagantsev conspiracy" will not stand scrutiny; the historians of Soviet poetry, and indeed the government itself, prefer to have the case forgotten.

Undoubtedly, there was a little band of conspirators in the northern capital who invested their hopes in the fall of the Bolshevik dictatorship. The conspiracy was named after Tagantsev only because his was the best known name among them, since his father, Senator and Professor of Criminal Law (1843–1923), was well known to every intellectual. Professor Tagantsev was Russia's outstanding authority on

---

[12] The information concerning Gumilev and the so-called Tagantsev Conspiracy is taken from the *Petrogradskaya Pravda* of September 1, 1921; the *Sotsialisticheskii Vestnik* of the same date; the memoirs of V. F. Khodasevich on "Gumilev and Blok," *op. cit.*, pp. 113–40; N. Gumilev, *Izbrannoe*, with Introduction and under editorship of N. Otsup (Paris, 1959); N. Gumilev, *Sobranie Sochinenii v Chetyrekh Tomakh*, G. P. Struve and B. A. Fillipov, eds., Vol. I (Washington, 1962), pp. vii–xliv; and personal letters to me from Boris A. Fillipov and from the Russian poetess Irina Odoyevtseva, writing from memory almost a half century after the events which she narrates in her letter.

Criminal Law, the author of the Code of 1903, an advocate of the abolition of capital punishment and the moderating of all punishments. But his son, V. A. Tagantsev, was not the ideological leader of the group.[13] This leadership came from a Professor Lazarevsky, who was vaguely accused of drawing up "a project for local self-government and monetary reform." In arresting the little group of intellectuals, the Cheka, as was already its custom, used the technique of "amalgam," lumping together all sorts and conditions of men with whom they wanted to settle accounts, or whom they wished to stop from vocally expressing criticism and opposition. Gumilev had been born in Kronstadt and was lecturing on poetry to sailors of the Baltic fleet at the time of the arrest. A number of Kronstadt sailors, including some who had been Communists until the Kronstadt rebellion, were seized in the dragnet. There were some Kadets (Constitutional Democrats), some Menshevik Socialists, some Socialist Revolutionaries and anarchists. Gumilev agreed with none of these, but to his interrogators openly pronounced himself a "convinced monarchist." Prince Ukhtomsky, a sculptor, was included in the "conspiracy" because he had "set up an organization for reporting abroad on museum affairs." (Under the totalitarian dictatorship then developing, even the location and fate of works of art was a state secret.) Among those executed were Tagantsev and his twenty-six-year-old wife ("as his accomplice"), Professor Lazarevsky, the geologist V. M. Kozlovskii, the sculptor Ukhtomsky, some Kronstadt sailors and their officers, some peasants and workingmen, and sixteen women—a total of sixty-one persons, one of whom was a poet. The Tsars had never dreamed of executing a dissident poet.

Nikolai Gumilev figured as Number 30 in the list of sixty-

[13] In all Soviet encyclopedias, Senator Tagantsev is treated very respectfully, and no mention is made of a "Tagantsev conspiracy."

one conspirators. *Petrogradskaya Pravda* gave these details concerning him:

> Gumilev, Nikolai Stepanovich, thirty-three years old, former gentry, philologist, member of the collegium of the "Publishing House World Literature," non-party, former officer. Participant in the Petrograd Fighting Organization, actively collaborated in the drafting of proclamations of a counterrevolutionary character, promised to link up with the organization at the moment of an uprising a group of intellectuals, which would actively take part in the uprising, received from the organization money for technical needs.

As a poet, Gumilev had always been a loner, an adventurer, and a wanderer. To him the test of the genuineness of a poet was his readiness to act out his dreams. He was born in the Fortress of Kronstadt where his father was a naval doctor, had lived in Tsarskoe Selo, in Tiflis, in St. Petersburg, in Paris, in London, in Egypt, in Somaliland and Abyssinia (today Ethiopia) , had studied at the Sorbonne and in the St. Petersburg University, and since the age of eight had been writing poetry. His poetry grew better with each volume, and he wrote as well some of the finest critical and narrative prose in the Russian language. While still a gymnasium student he had married the lyrical poet Anna Akhmatova. Their only son, L. N. Gumilev, who has taught at the University of Leningrad as a specialist in Far Eastern Studies, knew persecution under Stalin not because of his father but as part of the harassment that Stalin's cultural boss, Andrei Zhdanov, directed at the "eroticism, mysticism, and political indifferentism" of his mother's poetry. L. N. Gumilev was freed from a concentration camp either in 1956 or early 1957 and, along with his mother's poetry, "rehabilitated." There are signs, of which more later, that his father, too, will be rehabilitated soon.[14] In 1918, on his return to Russia from abroad, Nikolai Gumilev and Anna Akhmatova were divorced. At the time of his arrest he was living with his second wife, Anna Nikolaevna Engelgardt, in the House of the Arts, and working as an editor with Maxim Gorky.

Gumilev was ideologically, or perhaps we should say theoretically, "a monarchist," as he stubbornly repeated to his inquisitors, but a monarchist in love neither with Tsar Nicholas nor with the autocracy. While in England he had noted how gentle the King was in his conduct of affairs, how democratic and secure the monarchy. Why is our Tsar, he asked himself, both so harsh and so insecure on his throne? He concluded that England's strength lay in her colonies, so, like the impulsive dreamer he was, he went off absurdly to Africa, to Abyssinia and Somaliland, to find his monarch a colony! His "imperialism" was as real as his "conspiratorialness." What he loved was not the actual monarch of Russia but the idea of monarchy. With a poet's sensitivity, he foresaw the fall of the reigning Tsar years before he fell. In 1910, in *Agamemnon's Warrior,* he wrote:

Burdensome, burdensome, shameful—
To live, having lost our king.

And in 1917, in *Gondla:*

Years of disaster followed
The end of the kingly race,
As freedom, that will-o-the-wisp,
Led us its merry chase.

In Africa, hot and bored, he had lived his poet's imperialist dream of the quest of a colony for his Tsar. In the same

---

[14] On the arrest and persecution of L. N. Gumilev, see the obituary article on his mother in the *New York Times,* March 6, 1966.

fashion, when war came he volunteered ["There are many ways for a man to live / But only one for a man to die"]. He was made an officer and decorated twice for bravery, but he found soldiering boring and was miserable in the army. Yet out of his misery came such songs as these:

Like thunderous hammer blows,
Like tides that never rest,
The golden heart of Russia
Is beating in my breast.

Gumilev made no secret, either, of his opposition to the Bolshevik dictatorship. He returned voluntarily to Russia from abroad after receiving a letter from Anna Akhmatova urging him that the place of a poet was among his own people, and his roots in his native tongue.[15] On his arrival in starving, freezing, culturally bleak Petrograd, he threw himself heart and soul into literary activities. "On politics," as A. Ya. Levinson who worked with him in the Institute of World Literature was to write after his death, "he said almost nothing: once and for all having rejected the regime with indignation and contempt, it was as if it did not exist for him."[16] But he served Russian culture and the Russian people with all his ripening powers. He gave lectures on writing and on literary criticism in Proletkult, Baltflot (the Baltic Fleet with Headquarters at Kronstadt), the Institute of the Living Word, the House of the Arts, the Institute of the History of the Arts, and other institutions. He translated poetry from French and from English, and retranslated through the

[15] It was the British literary critic John Cournos (now in his eighties) who carried the letter from Akhmatova to Gumilev. He gave an account of his mission in the *New Leader* (New York), November 22, 1965.

[16] Cited by Gleb Struve in his introduction to Vol. I of G. P. Struve and B. A. Fillipov, eds., *Sobranie Sochinenii* of N. Gumilev (Washington, 1962), p. xxxii.

French from Arabic. Under Gorky's patronage he published a translation of the *Rime of the Ancient Mariner* by Coleridge, ballads by Southey, and ballads from the Robin Hood Cycle. He translated French poets, and his own poetry often echoed their moods and thoughts. He reestablished the Tsekh Poetov (the Poets' Guild), publishing through them both poetry of his own and that of young poets who were inspired by him and found his enthusiasm for poetry contagious. From the French, he did into Russian the Arabic *Legend of Gilgamesh*. In the three years between his return from London and his execution, he revised and published a number of his earlier books of poems, including *Pearls* and *Romantic Blossoms;* he announced, but did not live to publish, revised versions of his *Alien Skies* and *The Quiver;* he issued volumes of new poems such as *The Camp Fire* (war poems), *Mik* (a poem of Africa), and *The Porcelain Pavilion*. In the year of his arrest he produced *The Tent* (new poems of Africa) and *The Pillar of Fire*. After his death appeared yet two other books which his supposed conspiratorial activities had left him time to write: a book of tales, *Shade From a Palm Tree* (1922), and a book of delicate lyrics, *To a Blue Star*. Clearly he was not a writer of the Gorky school, but the Curator of Culture had the wit to prize highly the contributions of Nikolai Gumilev to the golden treasury of Russian prose and poetry; like Blok, he was unique and irreplaceable. A single bullet could put an end to that teeming brain, but no amount of terror or sloganizing could replace it.

It seems clear from all the contemporary accounts of poets and critics—among them those of Nikolai Otsup, Vladislav Khodasevich, and Georgii Ivanov, who knew Gumilev well—that the Cheka sent an *agent provocateur* from Moscow, who presented himself as a "beginning poet" and asked for advice and criticism of his poetry. Gorky tells us this apprentice poet was "sent" to ensnare Gumilev and then give testimony against him.[17]

How the *agent provocateur* involved him in the "Tagantsev Conspiracy" is suggested by a letter from the poetess Irina Odoyevtseva to the writer of these lines, recounting the case as she saw it, a letter written to me about a half century after the events in question:

Once when I accidentally moved a box on his writing desk [writes Irina Odoyevtseva], I caught sight of the fact that it was filled with paper money. To my question as to where he had gotten so much money, he answered that the money was for the salvation of Russia, and, vowing me to secrecy, told me of the conspiracy without mentioning a single name.

That was in the Spring of 1921.

A few weeks later I found Gumilev, who was to move next day to the House of Art, engaged in a strange activity—he was pulling out and turning the pages of the books in his library, and there were a great number of them.

He explained to me that he had placed in one of the books a draft of a counterrevolutionary proclamation, and could not find it. I started to help him, but the two of us together could not find it. Finally Gumilev gave up the search. He left his library temporarily in his old room.

After his arrest, the Bolsheviks [that is the Cheka] made a search and they found the proclamation . . . which figures in the indictment.

To Gorky, as to all who knew him, it was obvious that this terrifically productive poet, lecturer, storyteller, and critic (his *Pisma o Russkoi Poesii* which he continued during this period were published after his death as a Russian *Ars Poetica*), this strange "conspirator" who crossed himself openly and ostentatiously every time he passed one of the churches

17 For a summary of these accounts, see Struve, *et al., op. cit.,* pp. xxxvi–xlii.

of Petrograd, was no more a conspirator than, when he went looking for a colony for his Tsar in Africa, he was an "imperialist." The Cheka found what they had planted: a packet of rubles and the draft of a manifesto. The *agent provocateur* knew where to find the draft even if the poet did not.

Gorky [Odoyevtseva's letter continues] tried every thing he could do to save Gumilev, and for that purpose even went to Lenin in Moscow. Gorky managed to get a cancellation of the order to shoot Gumilev, and for that purpose a telegram was sent to the Leningrad [Odoyevtseva forgets that it was still called Petrograd] Cheka.

But either the telegram was delayed or, more likely, the Petrograd Cheka made believe that it had come too late and hastily carried out the death sentence.

A provocateur in all probability was involved. I have my suspicions as to who it was, but I cannot make up my mind to give you his name since I do not possess any final proof of his guilt.

Gumilev did not give the names of anyone in his cell . . . and no one else suffered any punishment. He never concealed his anti-Soviet views, but assumed that he [and his activities] were too well known and they would not resolve to do anything to him.

Yet such was his sensitiveness as a poet that, as with the fall of the monarchy, so with the manner of his own death he seemed to have foreknowledge. In *The Pillar of Fire* (1921) he wrote:

Those are not pumpkins on the floor—
Each is a human head.
The blank-faced executioner
Chopped mine off too with a blow,
There it lies with the others
In staring, grinning show.

And in "Bonfire" (1918) he pictures a workingman bent on
consummating his execution:

He stands before his flaming forge,
An aging man of middle height.
His eyes have a submissive look
From blinking at the reddish light.
His comrades all sleep in their beds.
He alone wakes and will not rest,
Intent on fashioning the lead
That will fly homing to my breast.

One looks in vain in the bloodstained pages of tsarist
tyranny for a single case of the execution of a poet for
oppositional views. Pushkin sympathized with the Decem-
brists and circulated in manuscript poems in praise of freedom and opposition to tyranny, but all that happened to him
was that he was sent under not too onerous conditions to the
south of Russia, that the censors watched more closely what
he printed, and that Nicholas I, whose reign began with the
Decembrist mutiny, assumed a protective censorship over the
poet's published work. Gumilev is the first great poet in the
history of Russian letters whose very place of burial is unknown. As Irina Odoyevtseva has written:

And over his grave
There is neither mound nor cross,
Nor anything at all.

In 1922, when his drama *Gondla* was played posthumously
on the Petrograd stage, demonstrative cries of *Author! Author!* caused the authorities to prohibit its further showing.
Eager to have his execution and even his name forgotten,
they managed to publish histories of Soviet Literature and of
Russian poetry under Stalin without so much as naming
him. In 1930, while Lunacharsky was still active and editor-
in-chief of *Literaturnaia Entsiklopedia,* a five-column (two

and one-half pages) article was devoted to Gumilev. But in the large three-volume *Istoriya Russkoi Sovetskoi Literatury* (1958, 1960, 1961), Gumilev is an unperson; the *Great Soviet Encyclopedia* gives him eleven lines, the *Short Literary Encyclopedia* (1964) gives him forty-six lines plus bibliographical references. Yet even in the time of Stalin, Vladimir Alexandrovich Lugovskoy wrote (in a work published only posthumously in 1960) that he visited a group of Soviet youth at the Moscow Children's Theater and that these Moscow children, mostly "working youth," "had managed to get hold of a little volume of Gumilev; they were transcribing copies by hand of Gumilev's poems. . . ."[18]

Evgenii Zamyatin records in his *Litsa* how twice he chanced to travel by train at night from Moscow to Petrograd with Maxim Gorky immediately after clashes between Gorky and Lenin over lives he was trying to save. In both cases Gorky was in a black mood. On the first occasion Gorky told him, while puffing angrily on a cigarette, "For my intervention I got a reprimand from Lenin: 'It's time,' he says, 'for you to know that politics is in general a dirty affair, and it would be better for you not to get mixed up in these matters.'" The second occasion occurred shortly before Gorky left the Soviet Union. He talked of the poet Gumilev who had been shot by the Cheka.

He was a person alien both politically and in literary matters to Gorky's way of thought, but all the same Gorky had done all he could to save him . . . and had already managed to get a promise that the life of Gumilev would be spared, but the Petersburg government somehow learned of this and hastened immediately to carry out the sentence. Never did I see Gorky so angry as he was that night.[19]

---

[18] Cited in a letter of Boris Fillipov to *Encounter* (London), January 1966, pp. 93–94, on "Gumilev in Russia."

[19] Evgenii Zamyatin, *Litsa* (New York, 1955), p. 93.

Indeed, the reigns of Lenin and Stalin were bitter years for poets; they were the years, as Roman Jakobson has written, of the "Generation that Squandered Its Poets:"

Gumilev's execution, Blok's long spiritual and physical agony and his death, Khlebnikov's cruel privations and atrociously painful end, the premeditated suicide of Yesenin, and Mayakovsky. . . . Thus in the twenties of this century, at the ages of thirty to forty, perished the poets who inspired our generation, every one of them with a sense of hopelessness unbearably drawn out and acute, not only those who were killed or took their own lives, but Blok and Khlebnikov on their sickbeds, too, were casualties. . . .[20]

Gorky felt that his power to save had ended in three disasters: the arrest and frameup of the Famine Relief Committee, the death of Blok and of Gumilev. He became morose and sick at heart and looked for a way to leave the scene of his humiliating defeats. He had begun his mission with a veritable hail of demands for rations, heat, light, funds, employment, publication of classics uncensored, funds for publishing houses, innumerable plans, petitions, protests, demands, enterprises, achievements. And now his term as unofficial curator of Russian culture was ending in defeats, betrayals, even by Lenin as in the case of the Famine Relief Committee, and the thwarting even of commands issued in Lenin's hand. If Lenin, too, was becoming increasingly annoyed at his intervention in these "dirty affairs," what was there left for him but to go abroad? The Dictator helped answer the question for him. On July 9, 1921, he wrote to Gorky:

I am so tired that I can't do the least little thing. And you are spitting blood and you don't leave!! Verily, verily, that is conscienceless and irrational. In Europe in a *good* sanatorium you

[20] Cited in Zavalishin, *op. cit.*, p. 70.

will both cure yourself and do three times as many big things. Truly, truly. But here, here there is neither a cure nor things to do—only busy-work and futile *trivialities,* SENSELESS trivialities. Leave here, and get well. Don't be stubborn, I beg you.[21]

That settled it. Gorky no longer had any reason to stay.

Lenin nevertheless had cause to be thankful, and Gorky proud, of all he had done for Russian culture. Though it ended in an impasse and a second exile, the Soviet Government now had much to boast of because Maxim Gorky had abandoned his own writing to save the intelligentsia, the museums and monuments, the culture of the past and the creators and bearers of the culture of the future. All who value Russian culture, whatever their politics, whether Reds or Whites or Greens or at whatever part of the political spectrum they may stand, every Russian has reason to be profoundly grateful to Maxim Gorky for this.

[21] *Lenin i A. M. Gorkii: Pisma . . . ,* p. 169.

CHAPTER X

The End of a Friendship

Even while the two men were working together most closely, the friendship between Gorky and Lenin remained an uneasy one. In political matters, on not one thing did they see eye to eye. Indeed, Gorky had entered into the pact in the fond hope of influencing, even of transforming Lenin.

Enough of sitting things out [he had said to his intimates]. The socialist democracy ought to enter into the ranks of the Bolsheviks, and imperceptibly encircle them. We must try to influence them lest they commit irreparable stupidities.

But in the game of *Kto kogo?* the stronger will of Vladimir Ilyich would inevitably prevail, and the would-be encircler be encircled. Their correspondence is full of examples of the conflict of wills. Thus in January 1919 Gorky wrote "slyly":

Don't you think that now is a good time to renew the publication of *Novaya Zhizn?* If so, it would be a good idea for it to come out simultaneously with the Menshevik paper.[1]

When Gorky bombarded Lenin with reports on the terrible things he was seeing in Petrograd and with petitions of every description, Lenin sought to convince him that he was reacting "with your nerves" to the "inevitable" ills of the city.

[1] Lenin had promised that the destruction of freedom of the press was to be only provisional. Gorky wanted to show that this freedom was being restored, by the simultaneous licensing of his *Novaya Zhizn* and the Menshevik *Vsegda Vperyod* (*Always Forward*). Lenin's only answer to Gorky's letter was to propose to the VTsIK (All-Russian Central Executive Committee of the Soviet Government) that they shut down *Vsegda Vperyod*. For Gorky's suggestion see *V. I. Lenin i A. M. Gorkii*, p. 118; for Lenin's proposal to shut down the Menshevik paper, see *Lenin*, Vol. XXVIII, pp. 425–26.

You write that you see "people of the most varied strata." It's one thing to see, another to feel daily concern. The latter is what you are coming to feel more than anything else from these "remnants"—because of the fact that your profession is making you "receive" dozens of enraged bourgeois intellectuals, yes, and because of their living conditions.[2]

Yet sometimes Gorky's letters touched a hidden humane streak in Lenin's character, for he had never altogether succeeded in remaking himself in accord with his blueprint of what a ruthless revolutionary should be. And at times Gorky did convince him that the "remnants" and their preservation might prove useful to his regime, so that, however reluctantly, he gave his curator support.

There were times when Lenin tried to stop the flow of petitions and complaints by putting the famous writer to some other use. Thus a number of his letters urge Gorky to take a steamboat trip down the Volga with Krupskaya to make propaganda for the Soviet regime.[3] A revisit to his beloved Volga was a great temptation, but Gorky did not answer these letters; instead he stuck to his painful tasks.

There were moments when Gorky's proposals, or his actions (for he was given considerable powers in the field of publishing) were such as to drive Lenin into one of his rages, as when his curator wrote him: "Among the manuscripts I am sending abroad [for publication] are the autobiographies of Chernov and Martov." Nor was Lenin mollified when Gorky enclosed his own favorable reviews of these two "counterrevolutionary" autobiographies.[4]

When the pact between the two men finally broke down

---

[2] The letter, one long rebuke, is in *V. I. Lenin i A. M. Gorkii*, pp. 131–34.
[3] For such letters see *Leninskii Sbornik, (Leninist Miscellany)*, Vol. XXIV, pp. 315, 316; *Lenin*, Vol. XXXVII, pp. 454–56; Vol. XXXV, pp. 346, 347–50.
[4] Gorky's letter and the reviews are in *V. I. Lenin i A. M. Gorkii*, pp. 147–48.

for the reasons we have noted (Kronstadt, the arrest of the public members of the Famine Relief Commission, the deaths of Blok and Gumilev) , Gorky felt he had by no means completed his task of salvation of Russia from the famine and the loss of her intellectuals.

He did not agree with Lenin that he had been "doing busy-work concerning futile trivialities." He knew that famine still threatened the lives of tens of millions, and that the intelligentsia was still in mortal danger. How deeply he felt about this is revealed in a letter he sent to an American woman, Jane Addams, as soon as he was settled in Berlin. On June 10, 1922, in the second year of the famine, he wrote her:

> I have been informed that in America the opinion exists that the famine in Russia has already lost its threatening character and that the work of the organization of Mr. Hoover is quite sufficient for the salvation of millions of Russian peasants condemned to death by starvation.
>
> Permit me to say a few words on this matter.
>
> I think that the work of the Hoover organization in its sweep is a phenomenon never before known in history. Never before has any land in the world come to the aid of another land so magnanimously with such prodigality of forces and resources. The people of Hoover are truly courageous men; I do not exaggerate when I call them heroes. America has the right to be proud of her children who work so splendidly and fearlessly on the vast field of death, in an atmosphere of epidemics, savagery and cannibalism.
>
> This work, besides its direct object—the saving of millions of people from death by starvation—has yet another and in my opinion an even more important significance: it awakens in the Russian people exhausted by war a feeling of humanity, it resurrects the dream that had died, a dream of the possibility of the brotherhood of peoples, it realizes the idea of cooperative, friendly working together of nations.
>
> The European war—and after it the intervention and civil war

and their horrors—embittered the hearts of the Russian people. It is entirely understandable that there arose in the *muzhik* a negative feeling toward foreigners—no matter who they were. . . .

And behold—in the terrible days of death by starvation, in the days of complete helplessness, these foreign enemies appear as the saviors of the lives of millions of children; unselfishly and fearlessly they work and by their work they demolish in the Russian people the seething feeling of enmity and hatred.

You of course understand how important this is, what splendid results the Hoover organization may yield. In the course of time, in spite of everything, we will live and work as friends and brothers—glory to him who brings nearer this moment necessary for our happiness!

I return to the basic theme of my letter.

The famine has not diminished. The Hoover organization devotedly working on the Volga, cannot, of course, embrace the sweep of misery in other regions of the great Russian land. On the banks of the Black Sea—Odessa and the Crimea—millions of people also perish helplessly. The Germans are dying out, colonists of the south, cultured people, splendid workers. The Jews are dying out, a yeast necessary for inert Russia. The work-loving honorable Tartars are perishing and, of course, most of all the Russians, especially the children.

The famine is more important and more terrible than all that is said or written of it. Hundreds of thousands of desyatins of sowed land are destroyed by locusts. The locusts eat and the people suffer. . . . They eat the grain, the grass, the leaves, epidemic illness starts and cholera threatens. I cannot give mortality figures because I have my doubts about the accuracy of the count of the dying. The letters which I receive from everywhere portray a terrible picture. Everywhere exhausted by the starvation of the winter, people throw themselves with avarice upon the first growth of the spring and—it is clear to you what will follow from that.

Permit me also to call your attention to the question of the Russian intelligentsia—for the most part learned Russians. These are all mature or aged people, exhausted by years of weariness from their heroic work under conditions of cold and hunger. They are the best brains of the country, the creators of Russian science and culture, people more needed in Russia than in any other country. Without them it is impossible to live, as it is impossible to live without a soul. These people are a precious thing on a worldwide, general and human scale.

In all Russia there are only 9,000 of them—an insignificant number for so huge a land and for the cultural work needed in Russia. These 9,000 most precious people are gradually dying out, without having succeeded in creating those who should replace them.

I think what I have said is sufficient to arouse the energy of the friends of the Russian people who wish to help Russia to live through this accursed year.

I pay my respects to you,

M. Gorky[5]

From this moving letter it is manifest that his concern for the 9,000 intellectuals was even greater than his preoccupation with the universal starvation, for the intellectuals to him were "the leaven that leaveneth the whole lump" and would transform Russia. All through the second half of 1921 and the year 1922, living in Western Europe, he continued his double effort unabated. The record of his life after he left Russia is far from complete, yet from entries in *Letopis* and from his correspondence we can see that his days and his thoughts were filled with activities on behalf of the starving in general, and the scholars in particular. A few illustrations

[5] This letter was published for the first time in *Novyi Zhurnal*, Vol. 82, 1966, pp. 285–87. The letter is in the possession of Isaac Don Levine, who refers to it in his *I Rediscover Russia* (New York, 1964). Neither the owner of the letter nor *Novyi Zhurnal* was able to ascertain the name of the recipient but, Mr. Benjamin M. Weisman in his doctoral thesis on "American Relief in Russia" has shown that it was Jane Addams. He found that a good part of the letter was printed in the *New York Globe*, August 4, 1922. The Gorky Institute in Moscow has an authentic copy of it, but so far has shown no desire to publish it.

will serve to give some notion of the intensity of his activities.

In September 1921 he got 10,000 marks from Tübingen for famine relief, and he gave an interview to a correspondent of the London *Daily News* on "The Situation in Russia." In October he went with S. F. Oldenburg to the University of Helsingfors, which responded generously to his plea on behalf of Russian scholars. In November he wrote a plea "To The Generous Heart of America," which was published in the *Literary Digest*. In it he appealed for special funds to aid in the publication and translation of works of Russian scholarship abroad. On November 8, 1921, he had a letter in the Berliner *Tageblatt*, and later that month wrote to America again—to Jerome Davis, to John D. Rockefeller, Jr., to the Carnegie Foundation, to the New York *Herald*. His appeals were classless and free from demagogy; his name was magic; the responses were generous.

On December 6, the self-same Lenin who had called his activities "trivialities" wrote to ask him to appeal to George Bernard Shaw and H. G. Wells to go on lecture tours in America to raise funds for the Russian famine. Gorky enlisted Wells in this effort, but pronounced Shaw too cynical.

He agreed to write articles for an Austrian journal which was to pay 25,000 kronen per article into the relief fund, he got money from the port workers in Le Havre and Marseilles, from Spanish, French, and Italian intellectuals, from appeals in Argentina and Brazil, from the workers in the arts of Vienna. He published signed appeals in the *Neue Freie Presse* of Vienna; *Current History* in the United States; wrote on "The Intelligentsia and the Revolution" in the *Manchester Guardian*, and did a book with Fridtjof Nansen and Gerhart Hauptmann, *Russland und die Welt*, the proceeds of which raised large sums for the purchase of medicines to be sent by ship to Russia.

For a man who had been too sick to stay in Russia, his

activities while "taking a cure" were simply astonishing. The time spared from trying to save the lives of individual poets from the firing squad gave him energy for an amazing burst of literary activity as well, and made this among the best periods in his writing career. The year 1922 saw the completion of his *Memories of Andreev;* his *Memories of Chekhov;* his grim pamphlet on Russian cruelty, *O Russkom Krestyanstve* (On the Russian Peasantry) , suppressed in Russia; his autobiographical sketches, *My Universities* and *Pages from My Diary;* and several tales, sketches, and movie scenarios. At the same time, he read the works of young Russian writers, offering them criticism and advice, and sent out a steady stream of letters to distinguished Europeans asking them to become contributors to *Beseda,* for the magazine was intended to link not only Russian writers abroad with Russian writers in the Soviet Union, but both with all the best writers in Europe. The contributors' list sounded like a *Who's Who* in Russia, in emigration, and in Europe and America. Among those who accepted were Albert Einstein, Thomas Mann, Anatole France, Gerhard Hauptmann, Bernard Kellermann, Romain Rolland, Benedetto Croce, Upton Sinclair, Guido da Verona, I. P. Pavlov, S. F. Platonov, S. F. Oldenburg, Alexandra Tolstoy, Andrei Belyi. But this journal, so full of brilliant promise of a dialogue between Russia and Europe, was the cause of a new series of bitter clashes with Lenin.

Gorky carried on a prolonged guerrilla warfare, gentle at first, then increasingly angry, to get Lenin and the masters of the Kremlin to open the walls of the fortress in which they had imprisoned Russian writers, cutting them off from Russian writing abroad and from free access to the writings of Western Europe. Seven issues of *Beseda,* a quarterly, were published,[6] but not one writer inside Russia was permitted to

---

[6] The last was a double number called 7–8.

contribute a single article, story, or poem, and not one copy of the journal was permitted to be sold in Russia. It was Gorky's first taste of totalitarianism in the world of culture. He was prepared to make many allowances for Lenin's treatment of the Russian people, but not in the field of cultural freedom. "I will not contribute a single line to any Soviet journal," he wrote, "until *Beseda* is admitted." But the gates of the fortress remained closed, and the contest of wills continued.

Lenin became ill, Rykov took his place, "promising action," yet still no contributions came from Russia to *Beseda,* nor was distribution of *Beseda* permitted in Russia. Most of the prominent contributors who had lent their names had second thoughts. This was not the dialogue from which they could expect prestige and honor. Two years passed and the same question was still being debated among the rulers of Russia:

> On the question [wrote Gorky to Khodasevich]—a question of extreme urgency!—whether or not to let *Beseda* into Russia, an extraordinary conference, attended by numerous and wise men. Three voted for admission . . . all the rest said "Don't let it in—then Gorky will come back home." But he won't come back. He is stubborn, too.

In May 1925, a number of copies were finally admitted (or so Gorky told Khodasevich), but then the "wise men" reversed themselves, so that not one copy was put on sale—a foretaste of what is today called "cultural exchange," supposed by many to be a new invention.[7]

Gorky began to have a new appreciation of the freedom he

[7] For Gorky's accounts of this series of adventures in dialogue, see his letters to his co-editor, Khodasevich, in *Harvard Slavic Studies,* Vol. I, 1953, "The Letters of Maksim Gor'kij to V. F. Xodasevič, 1922–1925, With Notes by V. F. Xodasevič and an Introduction by Sergius Yakobson," translated and edited by Hugh McLean, particularly pp. 303, 326, and 328.

enjoyed in Western Europe: "How amazing it is that your letters reach me! [he wrote Khodasevich] Apparently mine also reach you. Evidently one must believe that England is the land of freedom."[8]

Contrasting the state of letters in Western Europe with the rigid fetters being clamped upon culture in Russia, he wrote Khodasevich on July 1, 1924:

You know what? Europe, or more correctly, its literature, is a remarkable and unique phenomenon in the world! It sees everything, understands everything, and can talk about everything courageously and honestly. It is something like an "all-seeing eye."[9]

We must mark such judgments of Europe and its literature on the credit side of Gorky's ledger, when we are reading his coarse and careless invectives concerning the same Europe written in his declining years inside Russia, under the iron rule of Stalin.

For nearly a half decade Gorky continued his unequal battle for cultural freedom in his native land before he succumbed to old age and loneliness. He grieved about "the anti-intellectualism they were introducing into Russian prose [so different from] the profound and original intellectualism of Russian poetry" [a medium so much harder to control].

He grieved about the joylessness of Russian life under totalitarianism, contrasting it with the innocent joyousness of Italian life, even under Mussolini:

People really celebrate here, believe me! Three thousand cannonades, two sets of fireworks, five orchestras . . . in honor of Abbot Antonino, who a hundred years ago bade a whale disgorge

8 *Ibid.*, p. 323.
9 *Ibid.*, p. 318.

a Sorrento boy, which the whale did. They began celebrating on
Sunday [May 24] and will continue until July 7. . . .

If there is a bit of humorous exaggeration in this account,
another letter is too close to tears for laughter:

You know, it is the holiday season here. Almost every day there
are fireworks, processions, music, and popular celebrations. And
at home? I think, and—forgive me!—I am overcome to the point
of tears and fury by envy and anguish and disgust and everything.[10]

Italy had been at war, too, and lost, and had had her
upheavals, but at least there were circuses and a bit of bread,
or pasta, while in the Russia he had left behind in 1921 there
had been neither.

The new rulers of Russia [he wrote gloomily to Galsworthy,
President of the International P.E.N. Club] cannot allow any
apolitical organization in Moscow, for they do not recognize any
person not infected with politics from the cradle.

The politicalization of every person and every aspect of
life—what was this if not a working definition of totalitarianism? In another letter he wrote:

For news that stuns the mind . . . in Russia Nadezhda Krupskaya and a certain M. Speransky have forbidden the reading of:
Plato, Kant, Schopenhauer, Vl[admir] Soloviev, Taine, Ruskin,
Nietzsche, L[ev] Tolstoy, Leskov . . . and many similar heretics.
And it is further decreed: "The section on religion must contain
only anti-religious books." All this, supposedly, is by no means
fiction, but is printed in a book entitled *A Guide to the Removal
of Anti-Artistic and Counterrevolutionary Literature from Libraries Serving the Mass Reader.*
 . . . I have written in "supposedly" above the line, since I still
cannot make myself believe in this intellectual vampirism, and I
will not believe it until I see the *Guide.*

[10] *Ibid.,* pp. 320, 329.

My first impression was so strong that I started writing to Moscow to announce my repudiation of Russian citizenship. What else can I do if this atrocity turns out to be true?

If you only knew, dear V.F., how desperately hard and depressing it is for me![11]

This letter is curious and complicated, for it shows the ability of Gorky to stage little dramas within his own spirit by which he sought to convince himself and others of things he knew were not so. While he was writing to Khodasevich that Krupskaya's barbarous order only "supposedly" existed, he actually had had a copy in hand for almost two months. S. G. Sumskii-Kaplun gave him a copy of the little book of instructions on the purging of popular libraries on September 14, 1923, and Gorky was writing his letter, in which he tried to persuade himself of his own civic valor (the renunciation of citizenship) and of his doubts about the very existence of the *Guide*, on November 8, 1923. Moreover, this was not Krupskaya's first but her second order for purging the libraries for the popular masses, for the booklet begins with this introduction:

Already in 1920 the Political-Enlightenment Section of the Council of People's Commissars sent out to the localities instructions for the examination of [library] catalogues for the purpose of eliminating obsolescent literature from the public libraries.

However, up to the present the reports of Political-Enlightenment organizations with rare exceptions have failed altogether to mention their work for the revision and purging of books from the libraries, and in some provinces it was necessary for the GPU to intervene to see to it that that task of purging was begun.[12]

11 *Ibid.*, pp. 306–07.

12 So far as I have been able to ascertain, there is only one copy of Krupskaya's circular existent in the West, presumably the one that Sumskii used for his article on it in *Sotsialisticheskii Vestnik*, and then gave to Gorky. The copy is in the B. I. Nicolaevsky Collection of books, documents, and

There were matters in which Gorky was more forthright with himself and with others and really showed the civic valor which he pretended to in this letter, but they were matters dealing with the fate of persons, not of books or journals.

One of Gorky's dreams had always been that of the unity in a single fraternal family of socialists of all varieties. On an international scale, this meant the reunification of the international socialist movement, now divided into a "Second" International, a "Third" International, and a number of parties which stood between them and were grouped for the moment into something derisively labeled the "Second-and-a-Half" International. Early in 1922 these three bodies gathered together to discuss conditions of reunification. Among the demands made on the Bolsheviks by the representatives of the other two internationals were the calling off of the terror against Russian socialists and workingmen, and the abolition of the death penalty. It had long been a tenet of the international socialist movement that capital punishment was a relic of barbarism, and Lenin himself had voted for the socialist resolution against capital punishment at an international congress.[13] But now, when Bukharin and Radek at the conference of delegates of the three internationals undertook to pledge that the death penalty would not be used against the leaders of the Russian Social Revolutionary Party, whom Lenin was about to bring to

---

archives, now at the Hoover Institution on War, Revolution and Peace. It is a printed pamphlet of twenty-two pages and it includes children's books, many of them classics of children's literature, books on philosophy, psychology, history, economics, ethics, religion, historical novels; works on civil rights, the inviolability of the person, the constituent assembly, democracy, other varieties of socialism; and even the earlier Bolshevik writings the promises of which had not been fulfilled, or whose tactical directives had been reversed. The evidence that Gorky had a copy when he wrote his letter is given in *Harvard Slavic Studies*, Vol. I, 1953, p. 307.

[13] At the Congress of the Socialist International in Copenhagen in 1910.

trial, he simply repudiated the pledged word of his representatives. In *Pravda,* April 11, 1922, Lenin wrote an article
entitled, "We Have Paid Too High a Price."

In my opinion [he said] our delegates acted improperly when
they agreed: (1) that the Soviet government will not render a
single verdict of death in the trail of the forty-seven Social
Revolutionaries; and (2) that representatives of the three internationals would be permitted to be present at the trials. . . .

At this point Maxim Gorky wrote to Lenin that he would
break off all personal relations if the death penalty were
enforced in the trial of these men. Nor did he stop with his
own protest. He got prominent intellectuals such as Anatole
France, who had helped with his famine relief campaign, to
join him in demanding a fair trial of leaders guilty of nothing but leadership of a socialist party that Lenin had out-
lawed (see Plate XVIII).

The trial, which began in May, was a grotesque caricature
of a trial. Vandervelde, Theodore Liebknecht, and Kurt
Rosenfeld were denied admission to the trial either as law-
yers or observers; the defendants were without legal repre-
sentation. But these were no frightened, tortured communists confessing to crimes they had not committed. One of the
twelve condemned to death, Abram Rafailovich Gotz, expressed the spirit of all of them when he said:

We have used this platform to relate the story of our activities
to the working classes. . . . If this avowal is fated to become our
last legacy we shall fulfill our duty as revolutionaries to the bitter
end. Yes, it is true that we have had no compact with victory and
we must therefore now pay the penalty of a pact with death. . . .
I am not sure whether it is life or death that fate holds in store
for us. If it be death, we shall die like revolutionaries, looking
death straight in the face. If it be life, we shall work as before,

straining every effort in the interests of the working class and of socialism. . . .[14]

The chief prosecutor at the trial was Krylenko, himself one day to cringe and confess impossible monstrosities in the prisoner's dock, with Vyshinsky and Yezhov as his prosecutors. What made the trial of the Social Revolutionaries even more monstrous to Gorky was that Lenin compelled Gorky's old friend Lunacharsky to act as Assistant Prosecutor.

The shock in socialist circles in Western Europe was so great, the storm of protest so powerful—even in the Russian Communist Party where Bukharin led the protestors—that Lenin hit upon the cruel expedient of suspending the execution of the death sentence temporarily, and notifying the twelve condemned that it would be carried out if ever the Social Revolutionary Party, or any of its members at liberty, carried out a single act against Lenin's power and government. Wladimir Woytinsky, in his youth a Leninist, wrote the indictment of Lenin's act in these words:

This trial, which has touched to the quick the conscience of the civilized world and has united in an outburst of protest all tendencies of socialist and democratic thought, has concluded with a monstrous verdict.

Twelve men who have sacrificed their lives to the cause of the Russian Revolution and international socialism have been condemned to death by a court pretending to be a bulwark of defense of the revolution and of socialism.

The noose is tied about their necks, but those who hold the rope have not yet tightened it. . . . What are they waiting for? Do they expect the party to which the condemned belong to abandon its struggle for the sake of their lives? No. That is not

[14] Wladimir Woytinsky, *The Twelve Who Are to Die*, foreword by Karl Kautsky (Berlin, 1922, in English, Russian, German and French).

what the Bolsheviks expect. They have simply chosen to postpone
the execution to a moment more suitable for them.[15]

"It will be enough that one single factory is burned down
or one Communist killed by persons unknown," *Pravda* said,
"for the condemned men to pay for it with their lives."
Actually, the twelve remained in prison for years, living their
living death, with the noose figuratively ever around their
necks, until the Stalin purges. Lenin did not have the will to
carry out the death sentences after all, even though the activities of the party of these men continued as before. It remained for his successor to put an end to their lives in his
universal blood purges which took the lives of more men of
his own party than of any other.

With Lenin's connivance, a great campaign was started
now against Russia's greatest "proletarian writer." On July 9
Gorky was attacked in the columns of *L'Humanité*. On July
11 Anatole France was attacked by *Izvestia*. On July 15 the
Rote Fahne attacked Gorky. On July 20 Demyan Bedny
published some satirical verses against Gorky in *Pravda*. On
July 21 resolutions were adopted against the novelist by the
Union of Petrograd Stenographers and Typists, and the
Printers' Union. A hail of similar resolutions followed. On
August 8 he was attacked in a Moscow meeting of representatives of a Commission for the Defense of Russian Culture,
and on August 11 in *Izvestia*. Later that month, a journalist
editing one of the provincial *Pravdas* had the clever idea of
giving as the main headline of the journal the caption
GORKY DEAD![16] It was a political death that was being
referred to; but actually it was a friendship that was dying.

Gorky had already written to his former wife, and to the
Permanent Secretary of the Academy of Sciences, that he was

15 *Ibid.*
16 Zamyatin, *Litsa*, p. 93.

about to return to Russia. But he changed his mind now, and made arrangements to live in Italy instead. And from the moment of the death sentence on the twelve Social Revolutionaries until the moment of Lenin's own death, Gorky wrote not one word to him, or about him. Though admiration and affection must still have had a place deep in Gorky's heart, as the portrait of Lenin written after the latter's death was to show, Maxim Gorky broke off all relations with V. I. Lenin. The letter announcing the break has never been published, but it is testified to in the memoirs of various persons who were close to Gorky.[17] In any case, the prolonged silence itself was eloquent. Except for the posthumous tribute, the long and troubled friendship was at an end.

[17] See, for instance, Victor Serge, *Memoirs of a Revolutionary, 1901–41* (London, 1963), p. 164.

XI

Epilogue: Gorky's Three Portraits of Lenin

Gorky painted three portraits of Lenin—the first in 1917 and 1918 when Lenin was seizing power; the second in 1920 when Lenin reached the age of fifty; the third in 1924, when he learned that Lenin was dead. The three portraits have many traits, even many precise formulations in common, but only the first and third, in my opinion, belong to literature. The first is written in anger, the third in eulogy. The second is strangely ambiguous, as if Gorky himself did not know the purpose of the portrait nor understand the mood in which he was writing. All three reveal the ambivalence of the uneasy friendship of artist and politician.

We have already examined the first portrait (in Chapter VI: The Poison of Power). Here we must recall its main features for, strangely altered, they reappear in the other two.

Lenin is already poisoned by the corrupting poison of power [Gorky wrote in 1917]. This is proved by his shameful attitude toward freedom of the word, freedom of the person, and the whole sum of those rights for the triumph of which democracy has been fighting. . . . On this supposed road of "social revolution" Lenin considers it permissible to commit every sort of crime. . . .

The working class cannot fail to understand that Lenin is only carrying out some sort of experiment on their hides, with their blood. . . .

Lenin possesses all the characteristics of a *leader*, among them such indispensable traits for leadership as the absence of morality and a genuinely lordly lack of compassion for the life of the popular masses. . . .

Such is the indictment contained in Gorky's first portrait.

In 1920, perhaps out of friendship, perhaps in return for some favor granted the Curator of Culture by Gregory Zinoviev, boss of Petrograd and chairman of the Comintern, Gorky did his second portrait of Lenin for the official organ of the Comintern, *Kommunisticheskii Internatsional* (1920, pp. 1927–1936). The occasion was Lenin's fiftieth birthday, so the article would seem to have been intended as a birthday tribute. Yet Gorky's sharp powers of observation, and his honesty concerning what he was observing and describing, compelled him to repeat, sometimes verbatim, many of the formulations of the indictment of 1917. Lenin, it is worth noting, thought the portrait was an Aesopian attack, a use of the language of eulogy to condemn him—and, in his own house organ! What Gorky himself thought he was doing we must leave to the reader to judge. In any case, condemning or eulogizing, the artist in all essentials remains true to what he observes and feels.

For me personally [Gorky begins] the role of Lenin as a transformer of Russia is less than his significance as a world revolutionary. He is not only the man on whose will history has laid the terrible task of plowing to its depths and turning upside down the variegated, lumbering, lazy, human ant-heap called Russia. His will is a tireless battering ram whose blows powerfully shake the monumental structures of the West and the millennial foundations of the disgusting servile despotisms of the Orient. . . .

I still think now—as I thought two years ago—that for Lenin Russia is only the object of an experiment, begun on a worldwide, a planetary scale. Earlier this thought, darkened by a feeling of pity for the Russian people, aroused me to indignation. But as I watch how the course of the Russian Revolution, as it spreads and deepens, awakens ever more powerfully . . . the forces capable of destroying the foundations of the capitalist system, I now find that if Russia is indeed condemned to serve as the object of an experiment, it is unjust to lay the blame for that upon the individual who is striving to convert the potential energy of the toiling Russian masses into genuine kinetic energy.

Each gets what he deserves—and that is just. A people who rotted in the suffocating atmosphere of the monarchy, inert and will-less, lacking a belief in itself, not "bourgeois" enough to be strong in its resistance, or to overcome in itself the beggarly, stubborn striving towards bourgeois well-being—that people by the logic of its talentless history ought obviously to live through all the dramas and tragedies obligatory for the existence of a passive people living in an epoch of bestial class war. . . .

The best that can be said for these equivocal words is that they are neither sound political analysis nor sound apologetics. No wonder Lenin saw in them an Aesopian repetition of the earlier indictment—particularly because, at that same moment, their author was republishing the original indictment itself in Russian in Berlin under the title, *Revolyutsiya i Kultura!*

When you listen to Lenin speaking [Gorky's defense continues] you feel that he believes unshakably in what he says, and how firm is his belief—the belief of a fanatic, but not of a metaphysician or a mystic. It seems that he is almost completely without interest in the individual human being, he thinks only of parties, masses, states, and here he is master of the gift of prevision, possessing the intuition of a genius thinker-experimenter. . . .

A Frenchman asked me: "Do you not find that Lenin is a guillotine that thinks?"

Only Gorky could have gotten such a chilling sentence into the columns of the *Kommunisticheskii Internatsional!*[1]

Next the author tries to picture the utopia for which, in

---

[1] 1920 No. 12, Cols. 1931–33. Cf. Gorky's own words concerning Lenin: "He speaks an iron tongue; the language of the axe." Col. 1930.

his fantasy, Lenin is striving. At this point, his sense of sober
and expressive style in Russian prose fails him altogether,
along with his sense of how Lenin's mind works. How do you
see the new world of Lenin? [he asks himself, and answers]:

Before me unfolds a grandiose picture of the earth, elegantly
engraved by the labor of free men into a gigantic emerald.[2]
Everywhere there are garden cities—sites of gigantic edifices.
Everywhere the forces of nature, conquered and organized by
man's intelligence, work for him. And he himself—at last!—is
really master of the elemental and the spontaneous.

Only this last formulation is characteristically Leninist,
for all his life Lenin detested and fought to control and
regulate the elemental and spontaneous, with the freedoms
and the unpredictabilities that go with it. At the outset of his
career as a Leninist, in his *What Is To Be Done?* (1902), he
wrote an entire chapter contrasting the *"Stikhiinost Mass i
Soznatelnost Sotsial-Demokratii"* (The Spontaneity of the
Masses and the Consciousness of the Social Democracy). Elemental spontaneity was something undesirable, to be fought
and controlled by social-democratic consciousness. In this
antithesis is the essence of Lenin's "utopia." Early in 1918 he
declared that the elemental, uncontrollable spontaneity of
the "million-tentacled hydra" of the peasantry, and the
workers affected by their mentality, were "the main enemy."
In 1922 and 1923, his last years in power, he reaffirmed this
view, adding grimly: "Petty-bourgeois spontaneity is more
terrible than all the Denikins, Kolchaks, and Yudeniches put
together."[3] This much at least of Lenin had rubbed off on
Gorky.

[2] The image of the earth as a gigantic emerald (*izumrud*, a word less
musical in Russian than in English) appeared in Gorky's writings before the
revolution, but then he did not attribute it to Lenin.

[3] *Lenin*, Vol. V, pp. 345–67; Vol. XXVII, pp. 303–04; Vol. XXX, pp. 155,
339. Cf. Leopold Haimson, *The Russian Marxists and the Origins of Bolshevism* (Cambridge, Mass., 1955); Wolfe, "Leninism," in *Marxism in the*

I do not think that I have ascribed to Lenin dreams that are
alien to him. . . . I cannot think of him as lacking these beautiful
dreams. . . . His personal life is such that in an epoch in which
religion was dominant Lenin would be regarded as a saint. . . .
Saint—this is really a paradoxical and comic word to apply to a
man to whom "nothing is sacred." . . . Saint Lenin—applied to
one whom the educated and cultured leader of the English con-
servatives, Lord Churchill, called the most ferocious of men!

But the honorable lord will not deny that churchly holiness
rarely excludes ferocity and cruelty, to which testify the bloody
feuds between the fathers of the church . . . the Inquisition, and
many other abominations. . . .

I am convinced that the terror costs Lenin unbearable suffering. . . . It is improbable, unbearable, to think that people
condemned by history to kill some for the freedom of others
should not feel torment that desolates their spirit. . . . All killing
is organically repugnant to me, but such people are [themselves]
martyrs, and my conscience never permits me to condemn
them. . . .

In these lines I have written of a man who was able fearlessly
to begin a general European social revolution in a land where a
significant percentage of the peasants wanted only to be satisfied
little bourgeois—and nothing more. This fearlessness many took
to be madness. . . .

There was a moment when my natural pity for the Russian
people made me regard this as madness too, almost as a crime.
But now, when I see that this people knows much better how to
suffer . . . than to work consciously and honestly—once more I
sing glory to the sacred madness of the brave.

And among them, Vladimir Lenin is the first, and the maddest.

Lenin was furious when he read this tribute and defense.
What he said in his protest to Zinoviev is not a matter of

Modern World, Milorad M. Drachkovitch, ed., (Stanford, 1965), pp. 76–89;
and Wolfe, "A Party of a New Type," in The Comintern: Historical
Highlights, Milorad M. Drachkovitch and Branko Lazich, eds., (New York,
1966), pp. 20–44.

record. But after his death his disciples chose to explain his anger by saying he was "embarrassed by the cult of his person."

Gorky's third portrait of Lenin is as moving as the first. The portrait of 1917 was inspired by Gorky's love of freedom and affection and pity for the Russian people, who were being subjected to a new tyranny in the name of freedom, and to a ruthless experiment in the name of the world revolution. Its picture of Lenin is Maxim Gorky's *J'accuse*. But the third portrait is written out of the author's grief at Lenin's death, out of his pride that even Lenin's enemies were now writing words of praise or reluctant tribute. It is written with love, at the death of a great man who has been the writer's friend. Yet even in this tribute to Lenin at his death, there is the strange ambivalence of a truthful portrait. Although with attempted justifications the substance of the earlier indictment reappears. Lenin's successors, with their hagiographical cult and their powers of pressure and censorship over Gorky's writing, caused him to modify this death tribute again and again. A variorum edition of this little article or pamphlet would prove extremely instructive as to its author's changing moods and the varying power of Lenin's successor and his cultural police to dictate to anyone writing on Lenin inside Russia under Stalin's sway. The most instructive variants are the first, written under the impact of the death of the leader and published in *Russkii Sovremennik* (No. 1, 1924, pp. 229–44), under the simple caption Vladimir Lenin. , and the final Stalinist version published in many languages in the early 'thirties as *Days with Lenin*, by Maxim Gorky.[4] It is from these two versions that all the quotations in the present work are drawn, and,

---

[4] English translations: *Lenin* (Moscow, 1931) ; *Days with Lenin* (New York, 1932) .

unless otherwise stated, the quotations are from the earliest
variant.

Gorky begins his obituary tribute with a touch of pride
that "the bourgeois press" in speaking of the dead leader was
compelled to recognize his genius: "Great, inaccessible, and
terrible does Lenin appear, even in death." It is clear that
the tone of such tributes, Gorky comments, is not one of
mere gloating at the death of a great and troublesome man,
but in that tone sounds the note of the pride of man in man.
This is a familiar note in Gorky's writing—as we know from
his *Lower Depths*—and he would have expressed it in his
tribute even if he had been unable to find an obituary article
in a "bourgeois journal" (in this case the *Prager Tageblatt*)
on which to base it.

Lenin was for me [Gorky continues] an amazingly complete
incarnation of will striving toward a goal that no one before him
had put for himself in practice. And more than that, he was for
me one of those just men, one of those monsters, semi-legendary
and unexpected in the history of Russia, men of will and talent
such as Peter the Great, Mikhail Lomonosov, Lev Tolstoy, and
their like. . . . For me Lenin is a hero of legend, a man who tore
out of his breast his burning heart in order to light by its fire the
way for people out of the shameful chaos of our time, out of the
rotting, bloody swamp of corrupting "statism."[5]
. . . His heroism was almost completely devoid of external bril-
liance, his heroism—something rare in Russia—was the modest,
ascetic devotion of the honest Russian intellectual-revolutionary,
sincerely believing in the possibility of justice on earth, the
heroism of a man who has renounced all the joys of earth for the
sake of the difficult labor for the happiness of men.

Next, as if unaware of what he is revealing, Gorky pictures
Lenin as having committed a kind of surgery on his own soul

---

[5] What the architect of the totalitarian state would have thought of this
dratribe against "statism" is not hard to imagine.

to make it conform to his blueprint of what the character of a revolutionary should be. This gives us the celebrated picture of Lenin's attitude toward music and its effect on his spirit:

One evening in Moscow in the apartment of E. P. Peshkova [Gorky's former wife] listening to sonatas of Beethoven . . . Lenin said:

"I know nothing better than the *Appassionata;* I am ready to listen to it every day. It is marvelous superhuman music. Always I think with pride . . . what marvelous things human beings can do!" Then screwing up his eyes, and grinning, he added sadly:

"But I cannot listen to music often, it works on my nerves, I want to say sweet stupidities, and stroke the heads of people who, living in this dirty hell, can create such beauty. But at the present time one must not stroke people's heads, they will bite your hand, it is necessary to hit them over the head, hit without mercy, even though in our ideal we are against using any violence against people. Hm, hm, our duty is devilishly hard!"

On this Gorky comments:

Yes, the duty of honest leaders of the people is superhumanly hard. It is impossible to have a leader who is not to one degree or another a tyrant.

Probably more people were killed under Lenin than under [Wat] Tyler, Thomas Münzer, Garibaldi. But then the resistance to the revolution headed by Lenin was more widely and more powerfully organized. And to that we must add that with the development of "civilization" the value of human life has clearly become lower, something indisputably testified to by the development in contemporary Europe of the technique for the extermination of men and the taste for that business. . . .

A man of wondrously powerful will, in all other respects he was a typical Russian intellectual . . . renouncing art with the logic of one of Andreev's heroes [who declared], "People live badly—that means that I also must live badly."

Here Gorky tells of Lenin's asceticism in the midst of the famine, giving an account of the simplicity of Lenin's personal life that brings to mind the aphorism of Bertrand de Jouvenel in his *On Power:* "To be completely acquitted of egoism by the generality, rulers need only affect a studied austerity. As if the real pleasures of authority were not quite other."

To which we must add, in agreement with Gorky, that Lenin's austerity was not "studied" but natural. It was an integral part of his "soul-surgery," the remaking of his character in the image of his blueprint for the "true revolutionary."

In both the 1920 portrait and the obituary article of 1924, Gorky compares Lenin to Peter the Great, a comparison which Lenin himself seemed to justify, for he wrote, "Our task is to learn state capitalism from the Germans, taking it over *with all our might,* not sparing dictatorial measures to hasten its adoption the more completely, just as Peter hastened the adoption of Westernism by barbarous Russia, not stopping short of barbarous methods in the struggle against barbarism."[6]

Once, while stroking the heads of some children [Gorky's portrait of Lenin continues], he said to me: "Their life will be better than ours; much of what we have lived through they will be spared. Their life will be less cruel." And looking far off toward the hills on which a village rested solidly, he added dreamily: "All the same, I do not envy them. Our generation has accomplished a task astounding in its historic importance. The cruelty of our life, imposed by circumstances, will be understood and pardoned. All will be understood, all!" And he stroked the children's heads gently, with light and considerate gestures. [This was said of the coming generation that was to know famine, Civil War, forced collectivization, forced industrialization, concentra-

[6] *Lenin* Vol. XXVII, p. 302.

tion camps, cultural dictatorship, blood purges. But Lenin never doubted that their lives would be better, happier, and free from cruelty.]

Life is organized with such devilish cunning [Gorky says by way of apology for his protagonist] that if one does not know how to hate, it is impossible truly to love. This in itself, this ambivalence in the soul, is what corrupts man to his very core, this law of love through the road of hate condemns life to destructiveness.

In Russia, a land where the necessity of suffering is preached as the universal means to "the salvation of the soul," never have I met, nor do I know a man who felt hatred with such depths and power as Lenin—hatred, disgust and contempt for the unhappiness, the woe, the suffering of men.

In my eyes these feelings, this hatred of the dramas and tragedies of life, elevated Vladimir Lenin to an especially high plane, a man of iron in the land where the most talented gospels have been written to the glory and the illumination of suffering. . . .

It may be that Lenin understood the drama of existence in a too simplistic fashion and believed it too easy to eliminate all the apparent dirt and disorder of Russian life.

Yet that doesn't matter! For me, especially great in him was this feeling of irreconcilable, unquenchable hostility to the unhappiness of people, his clear belief that unhappiness is not an irremovably fundamental constituent of existence, but an abomination that people ought to and must wipe out of themselves.

I should call this basic trait of his character fighting optimism. . . . It was precisely this that particularly attracted my spirit to this man—a Man with a capital M.

[Surely all this tells us more about Gorky than about Lenin!]

———————— [7]

In the years from 1917 to 1920 my relations with Lenin were far from what I would have liked them to be, but they could not have been otherwise.

He was a politician. He possessed to the highest degree that

[7] The breaks and the lines are in the original obituary portrait.

artificially but precisely elaborated rectilinearity of view which is necessary to steer so vast and heavy a vessel as leaden, peasant Russia.

But as for me—I have an organic disgust for politics and am a very dubious Marxist, for I find it hard to believe in the intelligence of the masses in general, and in the intelligence of the peasant mass in particular.

For greater clarity I should say that the fundamental obstacle on the road of Russia to Europeanization and culture is the fact of the overwhelming predominance of the illiterate village over the city, the zoological individualism of the peasantry, and the almost complete absence in it of social feelings. The dictatorship of the politically literate workers in close union with the intelligentsia would be, in my opinion, the only possible way out of the difficult situation, especially complicated as it is by war and still more by the anarchistic character of the village. I part company with the Communists on the question of the estimate of the role of the intelligentsia, among the number of which must be reckoned all the old "Bolsheviks," who have educated hundreds of workingmen in the spirit of socialist heroism and high intellectualism. The Russian intelligentsia—both the learned and the worker-intellectuals—were, are now, and will long remain the only work-horse to be weighted down with the heavy load of the history of Russia. Despite all the shocks and alarms experienced by them, the intelligence of the popular masses still remains a force demanding leadership from outside itself.

I know that for this thought I shall once more be laughed at by politicians. I know also that the wisest and most honest among them will laugh not sincerely but—out of duty. . . .

———————

[At the Eighth Congress of the Russian Communist Party, held in March 1919, Lenin had reflected after his fashion through the prism of his own more cynical mind the influence of Gorky's ideas concerning the use and support of the intelligentsia. Gorky quotes his words now with pride:]

This question [said Lenin to the Congress] ought to be settled with complete definiteness. We can only construct Communism when the means of bourgeois science and technology make it more accessible to the masses. But for that we need to take the apparatus of the bourgeoisie, need to attract to our work all the specialists. Without bourgeois specialists it is impossible to raise the level of the productive forces. We must surround [the bourgeois intellectuals] with the atmosphere of comradely collaboration, with workers' commissars, communists [i.e. as overseers] put them in such a situation that they cannot break away, but we must give them the opportunity to work better than under the capitalists, for this stratum, educated by the bourgeoisie, will not begin to work otherwise. It is impossible to force an entire stratum to work under the cudgel. The bourgeois specialists are accustomed to cultural work, they have carried it on within the framework of the bourgeois order, i.e. they enriched the bourgeoisie with enormous material undertakings and in insignificant doses gave of their cultural work to the proletariat. But all the same they did advance culture in this, their profession. To the extent that they see that the working class not only values their culture but also aids in bringing it to the masses, they will change their attitude toward us. Then they will be won morally and not only estranged politically from the bourgeoisie. We must attract them into our apparatus, and for that we need sometimes to make sacrifices too. In our relations with the specialists we ought not limit ourselves to the policy of petty nagging.

"We must give them as far as possible better conditions for their existence. That will be the best policy. . . ."

[Lenin thus in effect took over Gorky's policy, but coarsened it from one of reverence and respect to one of genteel bribery.]

. . . Vladimir Lenin [Gorky continues] was a man who contrived to prevent people from living their customary life as no one before him was ever able to do.

I do not know which he aroused more: love or hatred. The hatred for him is nakedly and disgustingly clear, its blue pestilential stain shines clearly everywhere.

But I fear that even the love for Lenin in the case of many is only the dark faith of the exhausted and despairing people in a miracle maker, the love which awaits a miracle but does nothing to incarnate its strength in the body of life. . . .

———

It often happened that I spoke with Lenin of the cruelty of revolutionary tactics and ways of life.

What do you expect?"—he asked in wonder and anger. "Is humanism possible in such an unheard of ferocious struggle? . . ."

"By what measure do you measure the quantity of necessary and unnecessary blows in a fight?"—he asked me once after a hot exchange of words. To this simple question I could only answer poetically. I think there is no other answer. . . .

Once I asked him: "Does it only seem so to me, or do you really feel sorry for people?"

"For the clever ones I feel sorry. There are few clever people among us. We as a people are for the most part of a talented but lazy intelligence. The intelligent Russian is almost always a Jew or a person with a touch of Jewish blood in him."[8]

[8] In all editions of Gorky's *Memories of Lenin* or *Days with Lenin* published under Stalin and Khrushchev, as well as in the various editions of Gorky's *Collected Works*, this remark of Lenin concerning the role of the Jews in Russian intelligence is studiously omitted. So too, Gorky's article, later published in Berne as a pamphlet, *The Black Hundred Pogromists*, was omitted from the Academy Edition of the *Collected Works*. Gorky's lecture, "On the Jews," delivered in New York in Grand Central Palace on April 25, 1906, and his letter "On Zionism," published together as a pamphlet by *Pravda* in 1907, are also missing from his thirty-volume *Collected Works*. The same is true of his thirty-page preface to *The Legend of Ahasuerus, The Wandering Jew* (Petrograd: Grzhebin, 1919); his pamphlet *On the Jews* (published by the Petrograd Soviet of Workers and Peasants' Deputies in 1919); his *Protest against Society*, published in Berlin by Steinitz; his report to the Russian Association for the Study of Jewish Life, published in *Letopis*, of which he was the editor, in January 1916; his article on the Jewish writer Bialik, originally published in *Evreiskaya Zhizn* (*Jewish Life*) in 1916; his

Often I heard his praise of comrades. Even of those who, according to rumor, did not supposedly enjoy his personal sympathy, Lenin was able to speak with proper praise of their energy.

Surprised by his favorable judgment of one of these comrades, I made the remark that for many this appreciation would be unexpected.

"Yes, yes, I know! There are those who lie about my relations with him. Many lies are told, and it seems especially many about me and Trotsky."

Banging his hand on his desk he said:

"And I should like them to show me another comrade who is capable of organizing in a single year an almost model army, yes, and at the same time, able to win the respect of military specialists. But we have such a person. We have everything [in our country]! And miracles will occur!"[9]

Vladimir Lenin awakened Russia and now it will not fall asleep again. . . .

Vladimir Lenin, a great, a real Man of this world, is dead. His death was a grievous blow in the heart of those who knew him, a very heavy blow.

But the crossing of the dark border of death has served only to bring out more clearly his significance in the eyes of the entire world.

And if the dark cloud of hatred toward him, the cloud of lies and slanders around his name had been even more dense, it

---

article on the Kishinev Pogrom first published in *Osvobozhdeniye* in the early 1900s and republished by him in *Revolyutisionnaya Rossiya;* as well as a number of articles which he published in anthologies. Boris Souvarine has made a study of these omissions in *Dissent,* (Winter 1965) , basing his observations on an incomplete list of omissions drawn up by Leon Bernstein of the Bund, who was studying censorship of Gorky by the Gorky Institute of World Literature, the Academy of Sciences, and Lenin's heirs. We leave it to the reader to draw his own conclusions concerning this method of editing a great writer's *Collected Works.*

[9] This passage also was cut by Lenin's faithful disciples out of Gorky's *Collected Works* and his *V. I. Lenin* (Moscow, 1931) and *Days with Lenin* (New York, 1932) .

would be all the same: there are no forces which could darken the torch raised by Lenin in the spiritual darkness of a world that was going mad.

And there has not been a man who like him has really deserved the world's eternal memory.

In the end, what wins out all the same is that which is honest and right that a man does, that without which he would not be a man.

This strange and challenging ending, which has in it more of the spirit of Gorky than of Lenin, was changed in the later Stalinist rendering to read:

Vladimir Lenin is dead. But the heirs of his thought and his will are alive. They live and are carrying on his work which is more victorious than anything else in the history of mankind.

Not only the thought but even the style of this new ending is alien to Gorky.

The strange thing about these three portraits, the first an indictment, the second and third eulogies, is that all three make the same points:

1. Lenin is a man of wondrously powerful iron will.

2. He has striven to force the Russian people to do what no one has tried to put in practice before him.

3. To impose his will, he has contrived to prevent them from living their customary lives or realizing their own simpler desires.

4. He has used them in conformity with his will as an instrument of an experiment—through a backward, unready, and unwilling people to bring about a world revolution.

5. This experiment has cost the lives of more people than any previous revolution in history, and bespeaks a ruthlessness which the first portrait ascribes to "lordly indifference," the second to a "complete lack of interest in the individual

human being" by one who "thinks only of parties, masses, states," and the third to "the law of love through the road of hate." That thus in eulogy as in indictment the artist should make the same essential points testifies to his faithfulness to himself as artist and observer of his subject.

Maxim Gorky had been looking for "a man with a true and living faith," Lenin for an artist who would faithfully, accurately, and exclusively serve the Party and its ideology through his art—a man whose work, as Gorky angrily told Valentinov, should serve as a succession of "committee manifestoes" or artistic renderings of the Party line. The whole course of their stormy friendship testifies to the fact that neither really found in the other what he sought.

Selected Bibliography

WORKS BY MAXIM GORKY

Sobranie sochinenii. St. Petersburg, 1900–1910. Vols. I–IX.

Sobranie sochinenii. Petrograd, 1914–1916. Vols. X–XX.

Sobranie sochinenii. Berlin, 1923–1924. 22 vols.

Sobranie sochinenii. Moscow/Leningrad, 1924–1929. 22 vols.

Sobranie sochinenii. Moscow–Leningrad, 1928–1930. Vols. I–XXIII.

Sobranie sochinenii, 2d edition. Moscow/Leningrad, 1933–1934. Vols. I–XXV.

Sobranie sochinenii. Moscow/Leningrad, 1939–1949. Vols. I–XV.

Sobranie sochinenii. Moscow, 1949–1955. Vols. I–XXX.

Sobranie sochinenii. Moscow, 1960–1964. 18 vols.

Arkhiv A. M. Gorkogo. Moscow, 1939–1960. Vols. I–VII.
 Piesy i tsenarii. Moscow, 1941 (*Arkhiv Gorkogo*, Vol. II).
 Povesti, vospominaniia, publitsistika, stati o literature. Moscow, 1951 (*Arkhiv Gorkogo,* Vol. III).
 Khudozhestvennye proizvedeniia. Plany. Nabroski. Zametki o literature i iazyke. Moscow, 1957 (*Arkhiv A. M. Gorkogo*, Vol. VI).

Borba s negramotnostiu. Petrograd, 1920.

Byvshie liudi. Moscow, 1917.

Chelkash. New York, 1895.

Deviatoe ianvaria; ocherk. Petrograd, 1920.

Ein Jahr Russische Revolution, von Maxim Gorkij.* *Süddeutsche Monatshefte* (Leipzig/Munich). Vol. XVI, No. 1, October 1918.

Emelian Piliai. Delo s zastezhkami. Moscow, 1915.

Izbrannye rasskazy 1893–1915. Petrograd, 1921.

Makar Chudra. Moscow, 1892.

Mat. Moscow, 1946.

Na Dne. Moscow, 1923.

O Evreiakh.* Petrograd, 1919.

O russkom krestyanstve.* Berlin, 1922.

Prekrasnaia Frantsia. Stuttgart, 1906.

Prokhodimets. Legenda o Marko. Moscow, 1915.

Ranniia revoliutsionnaia publitsistika. S. M. Breitburg, ed. Moscow, 1938.

Razskazy. St. Petersburg, 1901.

Revoliutsiia i kultura.* Berlin, 1920.

Stati, 1905–1916. Petrograd, 1916.

Stati i pamflety. Leningrad, 1948.

Stikhotvoreniia. Vstupitelnaia statia, podgotovka teksta i primechaniia B. Bialika. Leningrad, 1963.

V Amerike. Stuttgart, 1906.

"V. I. Lenin." *Russkii sovremennik* (Moscow).* No. 1, 1924. Pp. 229–44.

Vaska Krasnyi. Petrograd, 1919.

Vospominaniya o Lve Nikolaeviche Tolstom. Berlin, 1919.

Zametki iz dnevnika. Vospominaniia. Berlin, 1924.

WORKS BY MAXIM GORKY IN ENGLISH TRANSLATION

The Black Hundred Pogromists.* Berne, n.d.

"The Children of the Sun." *Poet Lore* (Boston). Vol. XVII, No. 2 (1906). Pp. 1–77.

"City of Mammon" (City of the Yellow Devil). *Appleton's Magazine* (New York). Vol. VIII, 1906. Pp. 177–82.

* Titles marked with an asterisk are not at present included in the official collections of Gorky's works. For other works of Gorky presently excluded from the official canon but used in this book, see Plates 16, 17, and 18; and the text of pp. 9–12 and 137–38, and note 115.

The Confession. New York, 1908.

Decadence. New York, 1927.

Foma Gordeyev. New York, 1901.

Fragments of My Diary. New York, 1924.

In the World. New York, 1917.

The Judge. A play in 4 acts. New York, 1924.

Mother. New York, 1921.

My Apprenticeship. Moscow, 1962.

My Childhood. New York, 1916.

My University Days. New York, 1930.

"A Night's Lodging" (The Lower Depths). *Poet Lore* (Boston).
   Vol. XVI, No. 4 (1905). Pp. 3–64.

The Old Woman Izergil. Moscow, 1895.

On Literature: Selected Articles. Moscow, 1964.

*On the Bolsheviki.** London, 1918.

*On the Jews.** New York, 1906.

*On Zionism.** Moscow, 1907.

Orloff and His Wife. New York, 1901.

Orphan Paul. New York, 1906.

Reminiscences of Anton Chekhov. M. Gorky, A. Kuprin, I. A.
   Bunin, eds. New York, 1921.

Reminiscences of Leo Nikolaevich Tolstoy. New York, 1920.

Reminiscences of Leonid Andreyev. New York, 1928.

Seven Plays of M. Gorky. New Haven, 1947.

The Smug Citizens: A Dramatic Sketch. Boston, 1906.

Summer Folk. Boston, 1905.

Tales of Italy. Moscow, n.d.

Tales of Two Countries. New York, 1941.

Three of Them. New York, 1922.

Twenty-Six Men and a Girl. London, 1915.

V. I. Lenin. Translated from Russian. Moscow, 1931.

Days with Lenin. An American edition of *V. I. Lenin.* New York, 1932.

LETTERS

Gorkii i sovetskie pisateli: neizdannaia perepiska. Moscow, 1963 (*Literaturnoe Nasledstvo,* Vol. LXX).

M. *Gorkii i Leonid Andreev: neizdannaia perepiska.* Moscow, 1965 (*Literaturnoe Nasledstvo,* Vol. LXXII).

Perepiska A. M. Gorkogo s zarubezhnymi literatorami. Moscow, 1960 (*Arkhiv A. M. Gorkogo,* Vol. VIII).

Pisma k K. P. Piatnitskomu. Redaktor I. N. Uspenskii. Moscow, 1954 (*Arkhiv A. M. Gorkogo,* Vol. IV).

Pisma k E. P. Peshkovoi, 1895–1906. Moscow, 1955 (*Arkhiv A. M. Gorkogo,* Vol. V).

Pisma k pisateliam i I. P. Ladyzhnikovu. Moscow, 1959 (*Arkhiv A. M. Gorkogo,* Vol. VII).

Lenin, V. I. *Briefe an Maxim Gorki.* Vienna, 1924.

———. *Pisma V. I. Lenina k A. M. Gorkomu, 1908–1913.* Leningrad, 1924.

M. *Gorkii i A. Chekhov: perepiska, stati, vyskazyvaniia.* Moscow, 1965.

M. *Gorkii i V. G. Korolenko: perepiska, stati, vyskazyvaniia.* Moscow, 1951.

McLean, Hugh, ed. and tr. "The Letters of Maksim Gor'kij to V. F. Khodasevič, 1922–1925, With Notes by V. F. Khodasevič and an Introduction by Sergius Yakobson," *Harvard Slavic Studies.* Vol. I, 1953. Pp. 279–334.

Roland Holst, Henriette (van der Schalk). *Open brief aan Maxim Gorki.* Amsterdam, 1918.

V. I. Lenin i A. M. Gorkii: pisma, vospominaniia, documenty. Moscow, 1958.

Yershov, Peter, ed. *Letters of M. Gorky and L. Andreev, 1899–1912.* New York, 1958.

WORKS OF V. I. LENIN

Lenin, V. I. *Sochineniia*, 4th edition. Moscow, 1954–1966. These collected works were "complete" in 35 volumes in 1952, but since Stalin's death in 1953 other volumes have been added, volume 43 having come out in 1966 and volume 44 in 1967. There is no way of knowing whether the volume most recently issued is the final volume.

V. I. Lenin o literature. Sbornik statei i otryvkov. Moscow, 1943.

V. I. Lenin o literature i iskusstve. Moscow, 1957.

MEMOIRS

Balabanoff, Angelica. *My Life as a Rebel.* New York, 1938.

Bunin, Ivan A. *Vospominaniia.* Paris, 1950.

Chebyshev, N. N. *Blizkaia dal.* Paris, 1933.

Chukovskii, K. I. *Iz vospominanii.* Moscow, 1959.

———. *Repin, Gorkii, Maiakovskii, Briusov. Vospominaniia.* Moscow, 1940.

———. *Sovremenniki.* Moscow, 1962.

Fedin, Konstantin. "Gorkii. Iz vospominanii" in *Sochineniia.* Moscow, 1954. Vol. VI.

———. "Gorkii sredi nas" in *Kartiny literaturnoi zhizni.* Moscow, 1944.

Gippius, Z. (Hippius). *Siniaia kniga: peterburgskii dnevnik 1914–1918.* Belgrade, 1939.

Gruzdev, Ilia A. *Gorkii i ego vremia,* 2d edition. Moscow, 1957.

Khodasevich, V. S. "Gorkii" in *Nekropol: vospominaniia.* Brussels, 1939. Pp. 228–77.

Kuskova, E. "Mesyats soglashatelstva." *Volia Rossii* (Prague). Nos. 3, 4, 5, 1928. Pp. 150–69, 42–61, 58–78.

———. "Na rubezhe dvukh epokh: pamyati A. M. Gorkogo." *Posledniia Novostii.* June 26, 1936.

Kuskova, E. "Obezkrylennyi Sokol (K 35-letiiu raboty Maksima Gorkogo)." *Sovremennyia zapiski* (Paris). Vol. XXXVI. 1928.

Melgunov, S. P. *Vospominaniia i dnevniki.* Paris, 1964.

Nemirovich-Danchenko, V. U. *Iz proshlogo.* Moscow, 1938.

O Gorkom—sovremenniki. Sbornik vospominanyi i stati. Moscow, 1928.

Orlov, Alexander. "The Medical Assassinations: The Death of Maxim Gorky" in *The Secret History of Stalin's Crimes.* New York, 1953. Pp. 261–76.

Pozner, Vladimir. *Erinnerungen an Gorki.* Berlin, 1959.

Serge, Victor. *Memoirs of a Revolutionary, 1901–41.* London, 1963.

Stanislavskii, K. S. *Moia zhizn i iskusstve.* Moscow, 1948.

Trotsky on Maxim Gorky. *Byuleten Oppozitsii.* July–August 1936.

Valentinov, N. "Vstrechi s M. Gorkim." *Novyi Zhurnal* (New York). No. 78, 1965. Pp. 138–39.

Zamyatin, Evgenii. *Litsa.* New York, 1955.

Zelinskii, Kornelii. *Na rubezhe dvukh epokh: literaturnye vstrechi 1917–1920 godov.* Moscow, 1960.

BIOGRAPHIES

Alexinsky, Grégoire. *La vie de Maxime Gorki.* Paris, 1950.

Gourfinkel, A. *Gorki par lui-même.* Paris, 1964.

Hare, Richard. *Maxim Gorky—Romantic Realist and Conservative Revolutionary.* New York, 1962.

Kaun, Alexander. *Maxim Gorky and His Russia.* New York, 1931.

Levin, Dan. *Stormy Petrel: The Life and Work of Maxim Gorky.* New York, 1965.

Roskin, Aleksandr Iosifovich. *The Life of Maxim Gorky.* Moscow, 1944.

STUDIES ON MAXIM GORKY

Adamovich, G. "Maksim Gorkii." *Sovremennyia zapiski* (Paris). Vol. LXI, 1936. Pp. 388–93.

Amfiteatrov, Aleksandr. *Gorestnyia zamety. Ocherki Krasnago Petrograda.* Berlin, 1922.

———. "Maksim Gorkii" in *Vlastiteli dum.* St. Petersburg, 1912. Pp. 119–228.

———. "Novyi Gorkii" in *Sovremenniki.* Moscow, n.d. Pp. 79–112.

Balukhatov, S. D. and V. A. Desnitskii, eds. *Maksim Gorkii. Materialy i issledovaniia.* Moscow, 1941.

Chemeriskii, I. A. "Iz istorii klassovoi borby v 1921 g. (Vserossiiskii komitet pomoshchi golodaiushchim)." *Istoricheskie zapiski* (Moscow). No. 77, 1965. Pp. 190–208.

Chirikov, Yevgenii N. *Smerdiakov russkoi revoliutsii (rol Gorkogo v russkoi revoliutsii).* Sofia, 1921.

Chukovskii, K. I. *Dve dushi M. Gorkogo.* Leningrad, 1924.

Clark, Barrett H. *Intimate Portraits; Being Recollections of M. Gorky . . . and Others.* New York, 1951.

Desnitskii, U. *Maksim Gorkii. Ocherki zhizni i tvorchestva.* Moscow, 1959.

Ermilov, Vladimir V. *Mechta Gorkogo; osnovnye idei tvorchestva.* Moscow, 1936.

———. *O gumanizme Gorkogo.* Moscow, 1941.

Ermolaev, German "Nesvoevremennye Mysli." *Mosty.* Sbornik Stateik 50-letiyu russkoi revolyutsii. Munich, 1967. Pp. 177–199.

Filosofov, D. V. "Konets Gorkogo." *Russkaia Mysl* (Moscow). Vol. IV, 1907. P. 122 ff.

Khodasevich, V. T. "Gorkii (vospominaniia)." *Sovremennyia zapiski* (Paris). Vol. LXIII, 1938. Pp. 131–56.

Koltsov, Mikhail Y. *Burevestnik: zhizn i smert Maksima Gorkogo.* Moscow, 1938.

Letopis zhizni i tvorchestva A. M. Gorkogo. Moscow, 1958–1960.

Lunacharskii, Anatoli V. "Maksim Gorki" in *Siluety*. Moscow, 1965. Pp. 229–44.

———. *Stati o Gorkom,* 2d edition. Moscow, 1957.

M. *Gorkii i sovetskaia pechat.* Moscow, 1964–1965.

M. *Gorkii v epokhu revoliutsii 1905–1907 godov.* Moscow, 1957.

Merezhkovskii, Dmitri S. "Chekhov i Gorkii" in *Griadushchii Kham.* St. Petersburg, 1906.

Miasnikov, A. S., ed. *M. Gorkii v vospominaniiakh sovremennikov.* Moscow, 1955.

Mikhailovskii, Boris V. *Dramaturgiia M. Gorkogo epokhi pervoi russkoi revoliutsii.* Moscow, 1951.

Novich, Ivan Savelevich. *M. Gorkii v epokhu pervoi russkoi revoliutsii.* Moscow, 1955.

Plekhanov, G. V. "K psikhologii rabochego dvizheniia." *Sovremennyi Mir* (Moscow). Vol. V, 1907.

Shklovskii, V. *Udachi i porazheniia M. Gorkogo.* Moscow, 1926.

Shub, David. "Maksim Gorkii i kommunisticheskaia diktatura." *Mosty* (Munich). No. 1, 1958. Pp. 239–52.

Tager, E. B. *Tvorchestvo Gorkogo sovetskoi epokhi.* Moscow, 1964.

Volkov, A. *A. M. Gorkii. Stenogramma publichnoi lektsii, prochitannoi v Tsentralnom lektorii Obshchestva po rasprostraneniiu politicheskikh i nauchnikh znanii.* Moscow, 1950.

———. *Maksim Gorkii i literaturnoe dvizhenie.* Moscow, 1959.

Yuzovskii, Yosif I. *Maksim Gorkii i ego dramaturgiia.* Moscow, 1959.

Zavalishin, Vyacheslav. "Gorky and the Realists" in *Early Soviet Writers.* New York, 1958. Pp. 61–67.

OTHER WORKS

Bespalov, I. M. "Maksim Gorkii" in *Literaturnaia Entsiklopediia*. Moscow, 1930. Vol. II, pp. 643–56.

Gumilev, N. *Izbrannoe*. Paris, 1959.

———. *Sobranie Sochinenii*. G. P. Struve and B. A. Fillipov, eds. Washington, 1962. Vols. I–IV.

Instructions for the Examination of the Literary Holdings of Libraries and the Removal of Counterrevolutionary and Anti-artistic Literature. Circular issued by the Chairman of the Chief Political-Educational Apparatus, N. Ulyanova [N. Krupskaya]. B. I. Nicolaevsky Collection, Hoover Institution.

Kniga: Issledovaniia i materialy. Sbornik XII. Moscow 1966. Article by O. D. Golubev, "Publishing House 'Parus' (1915–1918), pp. 160–193.

Leninskii sbornik. Volumes and citations indicated in the relevant footnotes.

Lunacharskii, A. "Maksim Gorkii" in *Bolshaia Sovetskaia Entsiklopediia*, 1st edition. Moscow, 1930. Vol. XVIII, pp. 224–40.

"Maksim Gorkii" in *Kratkaia Literaturnaia Entsiklopediia*. Moscow, 1964. Vol. II, pp. 285–95.

"Maxim Gorky" in *Encyclopedia Britannica*. Chicago/London, 1956. Vol. X, p. 532.

Mikhailovskii, B. V. and N. P. Belkina. "Maksim Gorkii" in *Bolshaia Sovetskaia Entsiklopediia*, 2d edition. Moscow, 1952. Vol. XII, pp. 244–61.

Otchet pervoi vysshoi shkoly dlya rabochikh. Paris, 1910.

Woytinsky, Wladimir. *The Twelve Who Are to Die*. Berlin, 1922.

Index